101 Project Management Problems

and How to Solve Them

Practical Advice for Handling
Real-World Project Challenges

Tom Kendrick

AMACOM

American Management Association

New York • Atlanta • Brussels • Chicago • Mexico City • San Francisco
Shanghai • Tokyo • Toronto • Washington, D.C.

Library of Congress Cataloging-in-Publication Data
Kendrick, Tom.
    101 project management problems and how to solve them : practical advice for handling real-world project challenges / Tom Kendrick.
        p.   cm.
    Includes index.
    ISBN-13: 978-0-8144-1557-3 (pbk.)
    ISBN-10: 0-8144-1557-1 (pbk.)
    1. Project management.   I. Title.   II. Title: One hundred one project management problems and how to solve them.   III. Title: One hundred and one project management problems and how to solve them.
    HD69.P75K4618   2011
    658.4′04—dc22
                                                                            2010015878

About AMA
American Management Association (www.amanet.org) is a world leader in talent development, advancing the skills of individuals to drive business success. Our mission is to support the goals of individuals and organizations through a complete range of products and services, including classroom and virtual seminars, webcasts, webinars, podcasts, conferences, corporate and government solutions, business books, and research. AMA's approach to improving performance combines experiential learning—learning through doing—with opportunities for ongoing professional growth at every step of one's career journey.

Printing number

10   9   8   7   6   5   4   3   2   1

To all the good project managers I have worked with,
from whom I have learned a great deal.
Also to all the bad project managers I have worked with,
from whom I have learned even more.

Contents

Part 2: Initiation 53

Part 3: Teamwork 83

Part 4: Planning

Part 6: Control

Part 7: Tools   237

Part 8: Closing   247

Introduction

"It depends."

Project management problems frequently arise as questions, and most good project management questions have the same answer: "It depends."

By definition, each project is different from other projects, so no specific solution for a given problem is likely to work exactly as well for one project as it might for another. That said, there are general principles that are usually effective, especially after refining the response with follow-up questions, such as "What does it depend on?" For many of the project management problems included in this book, the discussion begins with some qualifications describing what the response depends on and includes factors to consider in dealing with the issue at hand.

This book is based on questions I have been asked in classes and workshops, and in general discussions on project management regarding frequent project problems. The discussions here are not on theoretical matters ("What is a project?"), nor do they dwell on the self-evident or trivial. The focus here is on real problems encountered by project managers working in the trenches, trying to get their projects done in today's stress-filled environment. These responses are based on what tends to work, at least most of the time, for those of us who lead actual projects.

Some problems here relate to very small projects. Others are about very large projects and programs. Still others are general, and include some guidance on how you might go about applying the advice offered in a particular situation. In all cases, your judgment is essential to solving your particular problems. Consider your specific circumstances and strive to "make the punishment fit the crime." Adapt the ideas offered here if they appear helpful. Disregard them if the advice seems irrelevant to your project.

Several general themes recur throughout. Planning and organization are the foundations for good project management. Confront issues and problems early, when they are tractable and can be resolved with the least effort and the fewest people. Escalate as a last resort, but never hesitate to do so when it is necessary. People will treat you as you treat them, so act accordingly. Good relationships and trust will make solving any problem easier—you really do get by with a little help from your friends.

Given the broad spectrum of project types and the overwhelming number of ways that they can get into trouble, it's unlikely that this (or any) book will effectively resolve all possible problems. Nonetheless, I hope that this book will help you to successfully complete your projects, while retaining some of your sanity in the process.

Good luck!

Tom Kendrick
tkendrick@failureproofprojects.com
San Carlos, CA

1. What personality type fits best into project management?

Depends on:

▲ The type and scale of the project
▲ Experience of the project team

Understanding Personality Types

There are a large number of models used to describe personalities. One of the most prevalent is the Myers-Briggs Type Indicator (MBTI). One of its factors describes a spectrum between introversion and extroversion. Projects are about people and teams, so good project leaders tend to be at least somewhat extroverted. Introverted project managers may find their projects wandering out of control because they are insufficiently engaged with the people responsible for the work.

A second factor is the dichotomy between a preference for observable data and a preference for intuitive information. Projects are best managed using measurable facts that can be verified and tested. A third factor relates to whether decisions are based on logical objective analysis or on feelings and values. Projects, especially technical projects, proceed most smoothly when decisions are based on consistent, analytical criteria.

The fourth MBTI factor is the one most strongly aligned with project management, and it describes how individuals conduct their affairs. On one extreme is the individual who plans and organizes what must be done, which is what project management is mostly about. On the other extreme is the individual who prefers to be spontaneous and flexible. Projects run by this sort of free spirit tend to be chaotic nightmares, and may never complete.

Considering Other Factors

Project managers need to be "technical enough." For small, technical projects, it is common for the project leader to be a highly technical subject matter expert. For larger programs, project managers are seldom masters of every technical detail, but generally they are knowledgeable enough to ensure that communications are clear and status can be verified. On small, technical projects, the project manager may be a technical guru, but that becomes much less important as the work grows. Large-scale projects require an effective leader who can motivate people and delegate the work to those who understand the details.

Good project managers are detail oriented, able to organize and keep straight many disparate activities at a time. They are also pragmatic; project management is more about "good enough" than it is about striving for perfection. All of this relates to delivering business value—understanding the trade-offs between time, scope, and cost while delivering the expected value of the project to the organization.

Finally, good project managers are upbeat and optimistic. They need to be liked and trusted by sponsors and upper management to be successful. They communicate progress honestly, even when a project runs into trouble. Retaining the confidence of your stakeholders in times of trouble also requires communicating credible strategies for recovery. Effective leaders meet challenges with an assumption that there is a solution. With a positive attitude, more often than not, they find one.

2. What are the habits of successful project managers?

Effective project leaders have a lot in common with all good managers. In particular, good project managers are people oriented and quickly establish effective working relationships with their team members.

Defining Your Working Style

One of the biggest differences between a project manager and an individual contributor is time fragmentation. People who lead projects must be willing to deal with frequent interruptions. Project problems, requests, and other imperatives never wait for you to become unbusy, so you need to learn how to drop whatever you are doing, good-naturedly, and refocus your attention. Project leaders who hide behind "do not disturb" signs and lock their doors run the risk of seeing trivial, easily addressed situations escalate into unrecoverable crises. Between urgent e-mails, phone calls, frequent meetings, and people dropping in, project managers don't generally have a lot of uninterrupted time. You may need to schedule work that demands your focus and concentration before the workday begins, or do it after everyone has left for the day.

This is a crucial part of being people oriented. Project leaders who find that they are not naturally comfortable dealing with others tend to avoid this part of the job and as a consequence may not stick with project management very long, by either their own choice or someone else's. Being people oriented means enjoying interaction with others (while being sensitive to the reality that some of your team members may not relish interaction as much as you do) and having an aptitude for effective written communication and conversations.

Referring to an Old List

As part of a workshop on project management some time ago, I challenged the participants in small groups to brainstorm what they thought made a good project leader. The lists from each group were remarkably similar, and quite familiar. In summary, what they came up with is that good project managers:

▲ Can be counted on to follow through
▲ Take care of their teams
▲ Willingly assist and mentor others
▲ Are sociable and get along with nearly everyone
▲ Are respectful and polite
▲ Remain even tempered, understanding, and sympathetic
▲ Can follow instructions and processes
▲ Stay positive and upbeat
▲ Understand and manage costs
▲ Are willing to "speak truth to power"
▲ Act and dress appropriately

Reviewing the results, I realized that the items from the brainstorming closely mirrored those of another list, one familiar to lots of eleven-year-old boys for about a century; that list is "the Scout Law." The version I'm most familiar with is the one used by the Boy Scouts of America, but worldwide other variants (for Girl Scouts, too) are essentially the same.

Effective project leaders are *trustworthy*; they are honest, can be relied upon, and tell the truth. They are *loyal*, especially to the members of their team. Project managers are *helpful*, pitching in to ensure progress and working to build up favors with others against the inevitable need that they will need a favor in return some time soon. Wise project leaders remain *friendly* even to those who don't cooperate, and they value diversity. They are also *courteous*, because the cooperation that projects require is built on respect. Project managers are generally *kind*, treating others as they would like to be treated. We are also *obedient*, following rules and abiding by organizational standards. Good project managers are *cheerful*; when we are grumpy no one cooperates or wants to work with us. We are *thrifty*, managing our project budgets. Effective project leaders also need to be *brave*, confronting our management when necessary. Good project managers are also "*clean*." It is always a lot easier to engender respect and lead people when we are not seen as sloppy or having low standards. (Actually, there is a twelfth item on the Boy Scout list: *Reverent*. Although it did not come up in the brainstorm, praying for miracles is not uncommon on most projects.)

3. I'm an experienced individual contributor but very new to project management. How do I get my new project up and going?

Depends on:

▲ Availability of mentoring, training, and other developmental assistance in your organization

▲ Your aptitude for leading a team and any applicable previous experience you have

▲ The experience of the team you are planning to lead

Getting Started

Initiation into project management often involves becoming an "accidental project manager." Most of us get into it unexpectedly. One day you are minding our own business and doing a great job as a project contributor. Suddenly, without warning, someone taps you on the shoulder and says, "Surprise! You are now a project manager."

Working on a project and leading a project would seem to have a lot in common, so selecting the most competent contributors to lead new projects seems fairly logical. Unfortunately, the two jobs are in fact quite different. Project contributors focus on tangible things and their own personal work. Project managers focus primarily on coordinating the work of others. The next two problems discuss the responsibilities and personality traits of an effective project manager, but if you are entirely new to project leadership you will first also need to set up a foundation for project management. Novice project managers will need to invest time gaining the confidence of the team, determining their approach, and then delegating work to others.

Engaging Your Team

Gaining the confidence of your contributors can be a bit of a challenge if you are inexperienced with team leadership. Some people fear dogs,

7

and dogs seem to know this and unerringly single out those people to bother. Similarly, a project manager who is uncomfortable is instantly obvious to the project team members, who can quickly destroy the confidence of their team leader at the first signs of indecision, hesitancy, or weakness. Although you may have some coverage from any explicit backing and support of sponsors, managers, and influential stakeholders, you need to at least appear to know what you are doing. It's always best to actually know what you are doing, but in a pinch you can get away with a veneer of competence. Your strongest asset for building the needed confidence of your team as a novice project manager is generally your subject matter expertise. You were asked to lead the project, and that was probably a result of someone thinking, probably correctly, that you are very good at something that is important to the project. Work with what you know well, and always lead with your strengths. Remember that "knowledge is power."

Seek a few early wins with your team, doing things like defining requirements, setting up processes, or initial planning. Once the pump is primed, people will start to take for granted that you know what you are doing (and you might also). Establishing and maintaining teamwork is essential to good project management, and there are lots of pointers on this throughout the book.

Choosing Your Approach

For small projects, a stack of yellow sticky notes, a whiteboard to scatter them on, and bravado may get you through. For most projects, though, a more formalized structure will serve you better. If possible, consult with an experienced project manager whom you respect and ask for mentoring and guidance. If training on project management is available, take advantage of it. Even if you are unable to schedule project management training in time for your first project, do it as soon as you can. This training, whenever you can sandwich it in, will help you to put project management processes in context and build valuable skills. Attending training will also show you that all the other new project managers are at least as confused as you are. If neither mentoring nor training is viable, get a good, thin book on project management and read through the basics. (There are a lot of excellent very large books on project management that are useful for reference, but for getting started, a 1,000-page tome or a "body of knowledge" can be overwhelming. Start with a "Tool Kit," "for Dummies" book, "Idiot's Guide," or similarly straightforward book on project management. You may also want to seek out a book written by someone in your field, to ensure that most of it will make sense and the recommendations will be relevant to your new project.)

Decide how you are going to set up your project, and document the specific steps you will use for initiation and planning. You will find many useful pointers for this throughout the problems discussed in the initiating and planning parts later in this book.

Delegating Work

One of the hardest things for a novice project manager to do is to recognize that project leadership is a full-time job. Leading a project effectively requires you to delegate project work to others—even work that you are personally very good at. Despite the fact that you may be better and faster at completing key activities than any of your team members, you cannot hope to do them all yourself while running a successful project. At first, delegating work to others who are less competent than you are can be quite difficult, even painful. You need to get over it. If you assign significant portions of the project work to yourself, you will end up with two full-time jobs: leading the project by day and working on the project activities you should have delegated at night and on weekends. This leads to exhaustion, project failure, or both.

4. What are the most important responsibilities of a project manager?

Depends on:
▲ Role: Project coordinator, Project leader, Project manager, Program manager
▲ Organizational requirements and structure

Overall Responsibilities

The job of a project manager includes three broad areas:

1. Assuming responsibility for the project as a whole
2. Employing relevant project management processes
3. Leading the team

Precisely what these areas entail varies across the spectrum of roles, from the project coordinator, who has mostly administrative responsibilities, to the program manager, who may manage a hierarchy of contributors and leaders with hundreds of people or more. Regardless of any additional responsibilities, though, the following three areas are required: understanding your project, establishing required processes, and leading your team.

Understanding Your Project

In most cases, regardless of your role description, you own the project that has your name on it. The project size and the consequences of not succeeding will vary, but overall the buck stops with you.

It is up to you to validate the project objective and to document the requirements. As part of this, develop a clear idea of what "done" looks like, and document the evaluation and completion criteria that will be used for project closure. A number of the problems in the project initiation part of this book address this concern, but in general it's essential that you reach out to your sponsor, customer, and other stakeholders and gain agreement on this—and write it down.

You also have primary responsibility for developing and using a realistic plan to track the work through to completion, and for acceptably achieving all requirements in a timely way.

Establishing Required Processes

The processes used for managing projects include any that are mandated by your organization plus any goals that you define for your specific project. Key processes for your project include communications, planning, and execution. For communications, determine how and when you will meet and how often you will collect and send project information and reports. Also determine where and how you will set up your project management information system or archiving project information. For planning, establish processes for thorough and realistic project analysis, including how you will involve your team members. Executing and controlling processes are also essential, but none is more important than how you propose to analyze and manage project changes. There are many pointers on all of this throughout the problems in the project initiation part of this book.

Setting up processes and getting buy-in for them is necessary, but it is never sufficient. You must also educate the members of your team and relevant stakeholders to ensure that everyone understands the processes they have committed to. Also establish appropriate metrics for process control and use them diligently to monitor work throughout your project.

Leading Your Team

The third significant responsibility is leading the team. Leadership rests on a foundation of trust and solid relationships. Effective project managers spend enough time with each team member to establish strong bonds. This is particularly difficult with distributed teams, but if you invest in frequent informal communications and periodic face-to-face interactions you can establish a connection even with distant contributors. You will find many helpful suggestions for dealing with this throughout the part of this book on teamwork.

Projects don't succeed because they are easy. Projects succeed because people care about them. Leadership also entails getting all project contributors to buy in to a vision of the work that matters to them personally. You must find some connection between what the project strives to do and something that each team member cares about. Uncovering the "what's in it for me?" factor for everyone on the team is fundamental to your successful leadership.

5. What is the value of project management certification? What about academic degrees in project management?

Depends on:
▲ Age and background
▲ Current (or desired future) field or discipline

Considering Project Management Certification

Project management certification has substantially grown in popularity in recent years, and some form of it or another is increasingly encouraged or required for many jobs in project management. The Project Management Professional (PMP®) certification from the Project Management Institute in the United States—and similar credentials from other professional project management societies around the globe—is not too difficult to attain, especially for those with project management experience. For many project managers, it is often a case of "it can't hurt and it may help" with your career. For those early in their careers, or looking to make a move into project management, or seeking a type of job where certification is mandatory, pursuing certification is not a difficult decision.

Certification in project management is also available from many universities and colleges. Although many of these programs provide excellent project management education, in general this kind of certification rarely carries the weight of certification from a professional society. University certification programs can provide preparation for qualifying for other certifications, though, and certification from well-respected universities may add luster to your resume within the school's local area.

For those project managers who are in fields where certifications and credentials are not presently seen as having much relevance, the cost and effort of getting certified in project management may not be worthwhile. For some, investing in education in a discipline such as engineering or business could be a better choice, and for others certification in a job-specific specialty will make a bigger career difference.

Even for jobs where project management certification is not presently much of a factor, though, there may be trends in that direction. A decade ago, few IT project management openings required certification of any kind; today for many it's mandatory, and similar trends are visible in other fields.

Considering Project Management Degrees

A related recent movement has been the growth in academic degrees in project management. More and more universities are offering master's degrees in project management, often tied to their business curricula. Such programs may help some people significantly, particularly those who want to move into project management from a job where they feel stuck or wish to transition into a new field. A freshly minted degree can refocus a job interview on academic achievements rather than on the details of prior work experiences.

Embarking on a degree program is a big deal for most people, though. It will cost a lot of money and requires at least a year full-time (or multiple years part-time while continuing to work). Before starting a rigorous academic degree program in project management, carefully balance the trade-offs between the substantial costs and realistically achievable benefits, and consider whether a degree in some other discipline might be a better long-range career choice.

Another factor to consider, as with any academic degree program, is the reputation and quality of the chosen institution. Some hiring managers might select a candidate with a project management certificate from a school that they know and respect over someone who has a master's degree from an institution they have never heard of or do not regard highly.

6. There are many project development methodologies. What should I consider when adopting standards such as the Project Management Institute PMBOK®?

Depends on:
▲ Organizational standards and requirements
▲ Legal regulations
▲ Your industry or discipline

Assessing Project Management Structures

Modern project management has been around for more than a hundred years, with many of the basic techniques tracing back to Fred Taylor, Henry Gantt, and others central to the "scientific management" movement of the early twentieth century. These basic project management processes have survived for so long because they are practical and they work. To the extent that today's bewildering array of methodologies, standards, and other guidelines for project and program management incorporate the fundamental tried-and-true principles, they can be of great value, particularly to the novice project leader.

Standards and methodologies originate from many sources: some are governmental, others are academic or from commercial enterprises, and many are from professional societies.

For many government projects, application and use of mandated standards—such as PRINCE (PRojects IN a Controlled Environment) for some types of projects in the United Kingdom or the project management portions of the Software Engineering Institute's Capability Maturity Model Integration (CMMI) for many U.S. defense projects—is not optional. For other project environments, though, the choice to adopt a specific standard is discretionary. In these cases, your choice will ideally be based upon analysis of the trade-offs between the costs and overhead of a given approach and the benefits expected through its use.

Commercial methodologies from consulting firms and vendors of complex software applications can be very beneficial, particularly in cases where large projects are undertaken to implement something complicated and unlikely to be repeated that is outside of the organization's core expertise. Methodologies that include specific approaches and details about handling particularly difficult aspects of implementation can save a lot of time, effort, and money. More general commercial methodologies available from consulting organizations and from the services branches of product vendors can also have value, but over time most organizations tend to heavily customize their use, abandoning parts that have low added value and modifying or augmenting the rest to better address project needs.

Standards from professional organizations are less parochial and can be useful in a wide variety of project environments. They draw heavily on successful established processes and are revised periodically by knowledgeable practitioners, so they also provide guidance for new and emerging types of projects. This can be both a blessing and a curse, however, because over time these standards tend to become quite bloated, containing much that is of value only in very specific project environments.

The emergence in the recent years of the Project Management Body of Knowledge (PMBOK®) from the Project Management Institute based in the United States as a worldwide standard is an interesting case of this. In fact, the "PMBOK" does not actually exist in any practical sense. The document generally referred to as "the PMBOK" is actually titled *A Guide to the Project Management Body of Knowledge* (or *PMBOK® Guide*). It is intended to be neither comprehensive (it's only a "guide") nor a methodology. It tends to expand with each four-year revision cycle a bit like a dirty snowball rolling down a hill, picking up new ideas that are tossed in, some with limited applicability and support, and shedding very little of the content of prior versions. Despite this, the many serious, well-meaning, and generally knowledgeable volunteers (full disclosure: including me) who undertake this gargantuan quadrennial project do as good a job as they're able to ensure that it is as useful as possible to the worldwide project management community. It was never designed, though, as a project management methodology. It lacks specific process information for implementation (again, it's the *PMBOK® Guide*); it does not address many specifics necessary for success for specific projects; and, in attempting to be comprehensive, it includes a good deal that may have little (or no) value for some projects. It also includes some content that contradicts content elsewhere in the guide because it is written, and rewritten, by subcommittees that may not agree all of the time. To use it as a foundation for effective project management in an organization would involve considerable work in documenting the details of relevant included processes, determining which portions are not relevant, and adding needed process content that is not included in the *PMBOK® Guide.*

Choosing Your Approach

In selecting a methodology or standard to use in managing projects, you must distinguish between the necessary and the sufficient. What is necessary includes general practices that are applicable to most types of projects most of the time. Whatever the source of guidance—a book, a training course, a structured methodology—there is likely to be a lot of this content. Standards and bodies of knowledge from academic sources and professional societies are strong in this area, but they often go little further. Successful project management in a particular environment requires a good deal that is unique to the specific project type, and sometimes is even specific to single projects. Commercial methodologies and mandated governmental requirements may flesh out the processes to include all that is needed for a successful project, but if not, the organization or individual project leader will need to consider what else will be needed and include it, to ensure that the approach will be sufficient.

Another consideration in all of this is the list of reasons not to adopt a project management standard. All structured approaches to project management involve overhead, so consider whether the additional effort represented by a given approach will be justified by realistic benefits (including less rework, fewer missed process steps or requirements, and more coherent management of related projects). If a complicated methodology involves filling out a lot of forms and elaborate reporting, estimate the potential value added for this effort before adopting it. Finally, before embarking on a significant effort to adopt a new approach for managing projects, ensure that there is adequate management sponsorship for such an effort. Stealth efforts to establish project management methodologies are easily undermined and tend to be short-lived, especially in organizations that have process-phobic management.

7. What are the key considerations when developing or revising a project life cycle? What should I consider when choosing between "waterfall" and "cyclic" (or "agile") life cycles?

Depends on:
▲ Project novelty
▲ Project duration and size
▲ Access to users and project information

Considering Life Cycle Types

Like methodologies, there are many types of life cycles, which vary a good deal for different varieties of projects. Life cycles are also often used either with, or even as part of, a project methodology to assist in controlling and coordinating projects. The two most common types of life cycle are "waterfall" and "cyclic."

A waterfall-type life cycle is an effective option for well-defined projects with clear deliverables. This life cycle has a small number of phases or stages for project work that cascade serially through to project completion. For novel projects that must be started in the face of significant unknowns and uncertainty, however, a cyclic life cycle that provides for incremental delivery of functionality and frequent evaluation feedback may be a better choice.

Assessing Waterfall Life Cycles

Although there are literally hundreds of variations in the naming of the defined segments into which a project is broken, all waterfall life cycles have one or more initiating phases that focus on thinking, analysis, and planning. The stages of the middle portion of a life cycle describe the heavy lifting—designing, developing, building, creating, and other work necessary to produce the project deliverable. Waterfall life cycles conclude with one or more phases focused on project closure, including testing, defect correction, implementation, and delivery. Whatever the phases or stages of the life cycle may be called, each is separated from the next by reviews or gates where specific process requirements are to be met before commencing with the next portion in the life cycle. Ensuring that projects meet the exit criteria defined within a life cycle is a good way to avoid missing essential steps, particularly for large programs where individually managed projects need to be synchronized and coordinated.

Waterfall-type project life cycles are often more of a management control process than a project management tool, and for this reason they often parallel the central phases in a longer *product development* life cycle that may include subsequent phases for maintenance and obsolescence that follow project work and often have initiation phases that precede the project. Whatever the specifics, when waterfall project life cycles are fine tuned to reflect good project practices, they help ensure that projects will proceed in an orderly manner even in times of stress.

Assessing Cyclic Life Cycles

Cyclic life cycles are useful for projects where the scope is less well defined. In place of a sequence of named phases, cyclic life cycles are set up with a series of similar phases where each contains development and testing. Each cyclic phase is defined to deliver a small additional increment of functionality. As with waterfall life cycles, cyclic life cycles are often set up in connection with a project methodology, commonly an "agile" methodology where the content of each subsequent cycle is defined dynamically as each previous cycle completes. For some cyclic life cycles, the number of defined cycles is set in advance, but whether the number of cycles is well defined or left open, the precise details of the features and functionality to be included in each cycle will evolve throughout the project; only a general description of the final deliverable is set at the beginning of the project. Software development is the most common environment where this sort of life cycle is applied, and on agile software projects each cycle tends to be quite short, between one and three weeks.

Choosing a Life Cycle

For general projects, a waterfall life cycle is typically the best fit. This approach generally provides a context for adequate planning and control with a minimum of overhead. Similar projects undertaken using the two approaches some years ago as a test at Hewlett-Packard showed that the traditional waterfall approach yielded results much more quickly and with less cost (durations were half and total costs were about a third). This was largely because of the start-stop nature of the cyclic method and the additional effort needed for the required periodic testing, evaluation of feedback, and redefinition. Agile methods and cyclic life cycles are effective, however, when the project is urgent and available information for scoping is not available. Using frequent feedback from testing as the project proceeds to iterate a sequence of software deliveries and converge on a good solution can be significantly more effective than starting a waterfall life-cycle project using guesswork. Some criteria to consider when choosing a life cycle are listed in the following table:

	Waterfall	Cyclic
Deliverable(s)	Well defined	Novel
Team size	Medium to large	Small
Project type	Large scale or hardware development, Fee-for-service, Construction, Research and development	Small-scale software development
User involvement	Infrequent	Constant

Establishing Reviews, Change Processes, and Metrics

Whatever your choice of life cycle, you will be most successful with strong and appropriate defined processes. Set up the review points at the conclusion of each phase in a waterfall life cycle to be no farther apart than about three months, and establish stakeholder support for the review process for each in advance. Clearly define the review requirements for the end of each cycle or phase, and use the review process to detect and deal with project issues. If significant changes are needed to the project deliverable, promptly initiate formal evaluation of the changes before initiating the next phase of the project. If the project objectives are threatened, investigate resetting the project's baseline. Gain stakeholder support at the close of each segment of the project before continuing to the next phase.

Life-cycle metrics are also an important consideration. When planning, estimate the duration and resource requirements for each portion of the life cycle. As each phase completes, determine any variances against expectations and against the results of past projects. Life-cycle metrics over time will enable you to determine the "shape" of projects—how much time and cost is consumed in each portion of a project. If a phase in the life cycle becomes too large, you may want to consider breaking it up into two or more new phases. If late-project phases are chronically longer or more expensive than expected, more analysis and planning in the earlier phases may be necessary. Metrics are also useful with cyclic life cycles. The duration and cost of each cycle should vary little, but you can and should measure the amount of incremental functionality delivered in each cycle. You can also use metrics to determine the number of cycles required to complete a typical project, and to set expectations more realistically.

8. How can I efficiently run mini-projects (less than six months with few dedicated resources)?

For less complex projects, the overall project management process may be streamlined and simplified, but it is still required. Planning, team building, establishment of minimal processes, and closure are all necessary.

Doing Fast-Track Planning

Small, short projects are often very similar to projects you have done before, so one very effective way to ensure a fast start is to develop appropriate templates for project plans and schedules that can be easily modified for use on new projects. If such templates are not available, schedule a fast-track planning session with at least part of the staff likely to be involved with the project, and as you develop the project documents, retain shadow copies that can be used as templates for future similar projects.

Small projects are also often cross functional and may have few, if any, contributors assigned full-time. To be successful with this kind of project, you must involve the sponsor and other key stakeholders with planning. Work to understand the reasons why the project matters, and during the planning communicate why the people who initiated the project think it is important.

Building Your Team

Without a full-time, dedicated staff, you may have some difficulty in getting reliable commitments. Work with each contributor to establish a good working relationship and mutual trust. Identify any aspects of the project that seem to matter to your contributors, including any work that they find desirable or fun, any learning opportunities that they might appreciate, the potential importance of the deliverable, or anything else that each individual might care about. Get commitment for project work both from your team members and from their direct management. Even on short, small projects, rewards and recognition are useful, so consider any opportunities you have for thanking people, informal recognition, and formal rewards.

Establishing Processes

The processes on small projects can be streamlined, but should not be eliminated. Change control can be relatively informal, and if the project is sufficiently straightforward it may even seem unnecessary. Nonetheless, you will be well served by establishing a process in advance to deal with any requested midproject changes. At least establish some basic requirements for requesting and documenting potential changes. Set up a review process that everyone agrees to in advance, and identify someone (ideally you) who has the authority to say "no."

Escalation is crucial on short projects where you may not have much authority. If you run into difficulties that you are unable to resolve on your own or require intervention to proceed, promptly involve your sponsor or other stakeholders who can get things unstuck. Problems on short projects can quickly cause schedule slip if not dealt with right away.

Communication may also be minimal on simple projects, but plan for at least weekly status collection and reporting, and conduct short periodic team meetings throughout the project.

Closing a Small Project

Projects without elaborate, complex deliverables are generally not difficult to close. The requirements are usually straightforward, so verifying that they have been met is not complicated. It may be a good idea as the project nears completion to do a "pre-close" with key stakeholders to ensure that the initial requirements remain valid and to avoid surprises. Work to ensure that sign-off at the end of the project is a nonevent.

Conclude even small projects with a quick assessment of lessons learned to capture what went well and what should be changed. Adjust the planning and other template information for use on future similar projects. Also, thank all the contributors and close the project with a short final status report.

9. How rigid and formal should I be when running a small project?

Depends on:
- ▲ Past experiences
- ▲ Background of your team
- ▲ All aspects of project size

Determining Formality

The short (and admittedly not very helpful) answer to this question is "formal enough."

As discussed in Problem 8, overall formality on small projects can be a good deal less than on larger projects, but it should never be none. One important aspect to consider is the complexity of the project, not just its staffing or duration. Even very small projects can be complicated, so establish a level of process formality that is consistent with the most daunting aspects of your project. Work with your team to determine what will be useful and keep you out of trouble, and adopt less formal methods only where your personal knowledge truly justifies it.

It is also best to start a project with a bit more process formality than you think is truly necessary; relaxing your processes during a project is always easier than adding to them once your project is under way.

Establishing the Minimum

Even for short, simple projects, define the objectives and document the requirements in writing. Other aspects of project initiation may be streamlined, but never skimp on scoping definition.

Planning may also be simplified, and you may not need to use elaborate (or in some cases any) project management scheduling software to document the project. With sufficiently straightforward projects, even scattered yellow sticky notes set out on a whiteboard might be sufficient. If your team is geographically separated, though, ensure that you have a project plan that can be used effectively by all.

Project monitoring may also be less formal, but collect and distribute status reports at least weekly, and maintain effective ongoing communications with each project contributor. Schedule and be disciplined about both one-on-one communication and periodic team meetings to keep things moving and under control.

Overall, watch for problems and difficulty, and adjust the processes you use for each project and from project to project to balance the trade-off between excessive overhead and insufficient control.

10. How do I handle very repetitive projects, such as product introductions?

Establishing Templates and Plans

As with very small projects, repetitive projects are more easily managed using detailed templates and plans that document the necessary work from past projects. Appropriate work breakdown templates that have been kept up-to-date may include nearly all the activities needed and reduce your planning efforts to minor additions and deletions, small adjustments to estimates, and assignment of ownership. If no templates exist, extract basic planning information from the documentation of past projects or initiate a fast-track planning exercise.

Assessing Project Retrospectives

Consider difficulties encountered by past projects and recommendations for change that came up during previous post-project analyses. Also identify any work that was added or new methods that were successfully employed on recently completed similar projects. Work with your project team to find changes that will improve the planning templates and make adjustments to them.

Incorporating Specific Differences

Finally, seek what is different or missing. All projects are unique, so no template will cover every aspect of a new project completely. Review the specific requirements to detect any that are at variance with those from previous projects. Add any necessary work that these requirements will require. Document completion and evaluation criteria, look for any that are new, and adjust the plans to accommodate them. Review all the work in the adjusted planning templates and verify that it is all actually needed. Delete any work that is unnecessary for this particular project.

Tracking the Work

Throughout the project, scrupulously track the work using your planning documents. Monitor for difficulties and respond to them promptly. When you find missing or inadequately planned work, note the specifics and update the planning templates to improve them for future projects.

11. How should I manage short, complex, dynamic projects?

Depends on:
- ▲ Staff size and commitments
- ▲ Nature of the complexity

Dealing with Complexity Under Pressure

Projects that represent a lot of change in a hurry have a potentially overwhelming number of failure modes. Part of the difficulty is compressed timing, often with a duration set at about ninety days to complete the work. When doing a lot of work in a short time frame, even seemingly trivial problems can trigger other trouble and cause the project to quickly cascade out of control. If the complexity is technical, thorough planning can help. If the complexity is organizational, strong sponsorship and exceptionally effective communications will make a difference. Whatever makes the project complex, a single-minded focus and disciplined project management processes will aid in avoiding disaster.

Maintaining Support

Work with the sponsors and key stakeholders to verify the business reasons for a "crash" approach to the project. Understand what the benefits of the deliverables will be and document a credible case for why they matter. Also determine what the consequences of an unsuccessful project would be. Use the business case for the work to secure adequate staffing and funding for the work, including a budget reserve to cover any contingencies as they arise. Also establish a process for prompt escalation and resolution for issues that are beyond your control, with a commitment for timely response and authority to take action on your own in the absence of a management decision within the defined time window.

Throughout the project, communicate frequently with your sponsor and key stakeholders, delivering both good and bad news without delay as the project progresses. Never allow small problems to develop into irresolvable quagmires, as they will rapidly become in high-pressure projects. Continuity of staffing is critical on this sort of project, so strongly resist, and enlist support from your sponsor to block, all attempts to change or to reduce the staffing of the project as it proceeds.

Planning the Work

On short projects, planning must be intense and effective. To minimize distractions, consider working off-site, and if you have any geographically distant contributors, do whatever you need to do to enable them to participate in person for project planning.

Engage your core team in gaining a deep understanding of all the project requirements, and work to develop a credible, sufficiently detailed plan for meeting them. One advantage of a short project is that the relatively short time frame restricts the number of options, so it may be possible to develop a solid, detailed plan in a reasonable time (assuming, of course, that the project is in fact possible). As part of the planning exercise, define the specifics of all testing and acceptance evaluation, and verify them with your stakeholders when you baseline the project.

Establishing Processes

On intense, fast-track projects, well-defined and agreed-upon processes are critical. Processes for communication, problem escalation (referenced earlier), risk management, and many other aspects of project management are crucial, but none is more important when executing a highly complex short project than the process for managing scope change. As part of initiation, establish a strong, sufficiently formal process for quickly assessing requested changes. Get buy-in from your project team and key stakeholders for a process that has teeth in it and a default disposition of "reject" for all changes, regardless of who submits them. Identify who has the authority to say "no"—ideally you as the project manager. Establish an expectation that even for changes that have merit, the disposition is more likely to be either "not yet," to allow the project to complete as defined and to handle the change as part of a subsequent follow-on effort, or "yes with modifications," to accept only those parts of the requested change that are truly necessary. Excessive change will guarantee disaster on complex, high-pressure projects.

Monitoring and Communicating

Finally, effective tracking and communication is essential. Aggressive plans must always be tracked with high discipline. Set status cycles to be at least weekly, and increase the frequency whenever things are not proceeding as planned. During times of high stress, schedule short five- to ten-minute stand-up or teleconference status meetings each day to stay on top of evolving progress. Handle problems and variances from plans within your team when possible, but do not hesitate to escalate situations where resolution is beyond your control, especially for any case that could endanger the success of the overall project.

Communicate status clearly and at least weekly, and do it more often when warranted. Use bulleted highlights in an up-front executive summary to emphasize any critical information in your status reports. Use "stoplight indicators" for project activities, and don't hesitate to name names and color items red or yellow whenever they appear to be headed for trouble. (Always warn people in advance, though, to give them a chance to fix things.)

Overall, strive to remain focused on your project and available to all involved with the work. Never skip status collection or reporting cycles, even when in escalation mode, and delegate responsibility to a capable member of your project team whenever you are not available.

12. How do I balance good project management practices with high pressure to "get it done"? How do I build organizational support for effective project planning and management?

Dealing with Process Phobia

In some environments where projects are undertaken, project management is barely tolerated as "necessary overhead" or, worse, discouraged altogether. Although very small and straightforward projects may be successful with little planning and no structured approach, as projects become larger, longer, and more complex this practice can become very expensive. A manager or project sponsor who prohibits good project practices by asking, "Why are you wasting time with all that planning nonsense? Why aren't you working?" will soon be inquiring why the project is well past its intended deadline and redoing some of the work for the third or fourth time.

Resistance to the use of good project processes can be from management above you, or from the members of your project team, or even from both. Although you may not be able to completely remove resistance from either source, there are tactics that can help.

Building Sponsor Support

Ultimately, the best tactics to use when approaching management about more formal project management processes depend on financial arguments. Although it may be difficult to "prove" that good project processes will save money, there are always plausible places to start. The best involve credible project metrics, especially those that are already in place, visible, and at adverse variance compared with expectations. If projects are chronically late, over budget, or otherwise causing organizational issues, you can do some root cause analysis to tie the performance metrics to poor project practices such as lax change controls or insufficient planning. Use what you learn to build a convincing case and negotiate management support for more structured project management.

Even in the absence of established metrics, you may still be able to find sources of pain that are obvious and might be relieved with better project discipline. You may be able to persuade your management with plausible estimates of potential savings or anecdotal evidence based on success stories either within your organization or from outside, similar situations.

When the view that formal project practices are mostly unneeded overhead is deeply entrenched, you may find that progress in gaining support is very slow and difficult. If so, proceed incrementally over time, seeking support for the processes that you believe will make the biggest difference first, and work to add more structure gradually over time.

Building Team Support

When you have difficulty encouraging good practices within your team, the best place to start is by identifying sources of pain and showing how better processes could provide relief. For example, many teams are reluctant to invest time in thorough planning, particularly when the contributors are relatively inexperienced. New project teams often have a strong bias for action, and planning and thinking doesn't seem to be either productive or much fun. The reality, though, is that the most important aspect of planning is ensuring that the next thing chosen to work on is the most important thing to work on, and this is only possible with thorough analysis of project work. Before the project can be completed, all the activities must be identified, and the choice between whether we do this up front and organize the work or do it piece by piece, day by day throughout the project should not be difficult. Thorough up-front planning not only sets up project work in an efficient, effective way, it also provides the project leader and the team with the knowledge (or at least a strong belief) that the project is possible. In the absence of a plan, the best we have are hopes, dreams, and prayers, none of which provides a particularly solid basis for project success.

Although it will appear to some that planning will delay the start of work and ultimately make a project take longer, it is easy to demonstrate that the principle of "Go slow initially to go fast later" is essential to efficient projects that get most things right the first time through.

Ultimately, gaining team cooperation for effective project processes relies on helpful mentoring and teaching. Good project managers lead by example, modeling the behaviors that they desire of their teams.

Resorting to Stealth-Mode Project Management

Winning the argument about whether project management processes are worthwhile depends on at least some open-mindedness on the part of others. When even your best arguments fall on deaf ears, you may find it necessary to take your processes underground. This is not a desirable way to proceed, but it's better than failing. Some project leaders do their planning, risk management, and other project analysis work at home or outside normal working hours. Over time, you will likely find co-conspirators who will help you, making your efforts both more effective and less lonely.

It is also possible that the obviously more successful management of your projects will be noticed. When you are approached to find out why, you may use this opening to engage in a discussion that can lead to more acceptance and support for better project practices overall, out in the open.

13. How does project management differ between hardware and software projects?

Depends on:
▲ Project size and complexity

Dealing with Tangible and Intangible Deliverables

The basic principles of project management are applicable to projects of any type, but there are some key differences worth noting between hardware development projects having physical deliverables and software projects that generate less tangible results. The specifics of the project life cycle may be dissimilar, and there are often differences in processes, such as those related to testing and scope change control.

Defining Life Cycles

Software projects, especially those with very novel deliverables that are relatively small, may elect to use an "agile" or cyclic life cycle, as discussed in Problem 7.

Hardware projects and larger software projects generally employ a more traditional waterfall-type life cycle, but the names of the life-cycle phases may differ. For product development projects, whether hardware or software, a typical life cycle will begin with one or more phases focused on definition and analysis, with a business decision to carry the project forward at a relatively early process stage. Software development undertaken on a fee-for-service basis, on the other hand, usually has more phases on the front end related to sales and proposal activities necessary to win the business. The business decision in this case is further along the sequence of phases and represents the decision by the customer to agree to the proposal and sign a contract. There may be only one or two phases subsequent to this decision point, to execute the contract work, and then to secure approval and payment.

33

Establishing Processes and Roles

With a well-defined hardware project, scoping changes are expected to be rare and the process for managing those changes is usually defined quite formally. Software projects also need good scoping management processes, but changes are inevitably more common, and (whether it is actually true or not) changes are considered to be less costly and disruptive to software projects. Particularly early in a software project, the process used to manage changes to the deliverable can be relatively informal, even after the baseline plan has been set.

Testing is another area where there are often differences. Software projects may have multiple interim deliverables that need to be tested and evaluated, so testing may be necessary throughout a software project. Owing to the nature of hardware projects, most testing tends to be scheduled shortly before project closure, including the unit tests of subcomponents of a complex system deliverable. Because hardware components may come together in a testable configuration only near the end, evaluation (except for that done as part of early feasibility investigation) is mostly done fairly late in the project.

For some types of hardware projects, the rate of technological evolution is relatively slow compared to software projects. Because of this, the technical expertise of a project leader of a hardware project tends to be deeper than that of those who lead software projects. For all projects, success depends on the subject matter expertise of the project manager, but software project leaders may be much more dependent on the specialized backgrounds of their team members. Because of this, and the increasingly cross-functional nature of software projects, effective software project leaders need to have especially well-developed people leadership skills.

14. How many projects can a project manager realistically handle simultaneously?

Depends on:
- ▲ Team size(s)
- ▲ Project complexity
- ▲ Project workflow continuity

Understanding Limits on Control

The number of projects that even an experienced, grizzled project manager can effectively manage is usually one. There are exceptions to this, but managing several simultaneous independent projects, where any or all of them might need attention at any time, often results in a loss of visibility and control, serious problems, and probable failure of one or more of them. Managing more than one project well requires either that the projects be small and simple, or that they not require uninterrupted effort.

Project leaders typically spend about 10 percent of their time interacting with each full-time member of their project team (or teams), so projects with about a dozen contributors will account for all the time that's available, and then some. Managing several teams of ten to twelve people working on separate projects can be successful through delegation of responsibility to leaders for each who can manage their assigned projects. Delegation such as this is a key tactic of program management, which focuses on management of multiple related projects.

Managing Very Small Projects

It is possible to manage more than one project if each is relatively small and the number of contributors in total is about twelve or fewer. Even if some of the team members are involved with more than one of the projects, you should be able to keep things in balance as long as cross-project timing and resource contention conflicts are minimal. Regard-

35

less of how small the projects are, though, for the sake of your sanity keep the total number of simultaneous projects below about a half dozen. You will find some additional suggestions for leading multiple small projects in Problem 81.

Managing Discontinuous Projects

Another case where managing more than one project may be feasible is where there are significant natural gaps in the work. For small projects that have a good deal of inherent "wait time" in their schedules, you can potentially manage a larger number at once. The maximum number depends on the complexity of the work and the proportion of work time to wait time. One very able and experienced project leader that I worked with who managed relatively complicated printing projects typically had between fifteen and thirty projects going at any given time, but of course most of them required only short bursts of attention about once a week.

15. How do I handle my day-to-day tasks along with managing a project?

Depends on:
▲ Whether you have a small or a significant number of other responsibilities

Determining Your Available Time

There are two aspects to this issue—the short term and the long term. In the short term, keeping up with your responsibilities starts with preserving at least a little slack time in your schedule. To ensure this, review your daily schedules at least a day or two out and protect a small amount of open time in both the morning and the afternoon for dealing with unanticipated needs. At the end of a day of back-to-back meetings, you will undoubtedly have a number of pending tasks, some of which will be late. Also, always check your schedule to preserve a bit of slack before accepting new meeting requests or other new commitments (or when planning new meetings yourself). When you must, say "no" to requests you cannot meet.

Longer term, balancing your responsibilities with your available time begins with a realistic assessment of your capacity. When your overall responsibilities exceed what you can reasonably get done, you will ultimately need to either delegate or eliminate some of your work.

For most project managers, the number of hours available in a week tends to be flexible, but it is finite. Exactly how you choose to estimate your capacity is up to you, but it is a good idea to begin with a maximum based on a combination of what you generally have done in the past, your personal preferences, and organizational expectations. Having determined your theoretical capacity, you should deduct about 10 percent or so to account for unexpected emergencies and personal time off for vacations and other time away from work. The remaining portion of your time is what is realistically available for formal commitments and responsibilities. (If you determine that fifty hours is your reasonable workload, you will need to reserve an average of an uncommitted hour per day in a five-day week.)

Assessing Your Project Management Responsibilities

Next, assess the amount of time your project management responsibilities require. As a general guideline, each contributor you regularly interact with will require about 10 percent of your time. In addition, you may have other related management responsibilities, such as filling out reports, assessing and reporting on job performance, managing outsourcing relationships, participating in project-related meetings, and routinely communicating with others outside of your team. When your overall project management responsibilities exceed 80 percent of your available time, you will probably have considerable difficulty keeping up with other responsibilities.

Prioritizing Your Other Responsibilities

List all your nonproject responsibilities, such as ongoing support and production activities, participation in task forces and organizational committees, and management requests. Rank order your list using assessment criteria such as:

▲ Value to the organization
▲ Time sensitivity and urgency
▲ Value to you personally when successfully completed
▲ Consequences to you personally when not successfully completed

It can be useful to determine both importance and urgency for these items. Just because a request is urgent does not always mean that it should be a high priority.

Balancing Your Responsibilities

Insert your project (or projects) into the sorted list just above any of your current responsibilities that are less important. Assess the time and effort requirements for all of your responsibilities that are listed above your project work (if there are any). If the aggregate workload represented by project work and your high-priority responsibilities exceeds your available capacity, you will need to delegate (or get others to delegate) enough of it to make accomplishment realistic.

If the difference is small, you may be able to deal with it yourself by delegating work for some of your key responsibilities or project activities. When delegating work, always seek willing owners, and for any responsibility where you remain ultimately accountable, remember that some effort will remain yours.

If the difference is large, you will probably have to escalate matters. You may be able to get your management to reassign some of your high-priority nonproject assignments to others. If this is impossible (or undesirable), you still may be able to get relief by securing help in doing the required work. If, despite your best efforts, you are unable to reduce the workload from your nonproject responsibilities, then you may need to offload some project work, modify the project baseline, or otherwise adjust the amount of time required to stay in control of your project. Part-time project management is rarely successful, however, so you should anticipate continuing difficulties if you are unable to realistically allocate a substantial majority of your time to project management activities.

After balancing your project and other highest-priority responsibilities against your capacity, you might have some residual lower-priority work at the bottom of your rank-ordered list. If so, you will need to delegate the work or get it reassigned to someone else. In cases where the work is truly unimportant, you may even get away with communicating your intention not to do it, and simply ignore it.

Reassessing Your Workload

The problem of creeping workload is perpetual. Shortly after you have successfully balanced your responsibilities and given yourself a reasonable chance of keeping up with your work, you are likely to find yourself again overwhelmed. Maintaining some slack in your short-range daily schedules will help, as will judiciously saying "no" to at least some requests that come your way.

It's also a good practice to reassess your workload against your capacity about once each quarter. Work with your team and management to delegate and reassign work to ensure that important commitments remain realistic. No one benefits when dates are missed, stress levels are excessive, mistakes are frequent, and people become burned out.

16. How do I develop and maintain supportive sponsorship throughout a project?

All projects need strong sponsorship. This begins with initiation, and extends through planning and execution. More than anything else, sustained sponsorship requires effective communication.

Establishing Communication

Throughout your project, maintain a basis for frequent, honest communication. In all communication with sponsors, emphasize factors that matter to them. When you're having a problem, stress why resolution is critical to them. When you have good news, highlight how your news benefits them.

Establish an effective communication plan for your project, and review it with your sponsor and key stakeholders. Obtain their buy-in and approval in support of ongoing two-way communication. Whenever possible, plan for face-to-face communication.

Initiating Your Project

As soon as you are asked to manage the project, begin a dialogue with your sponsor to validate the project objectives. Ask questions to determine why your sponsor kicked off the project and to answer the question "What's in it for me?" from your sponsor's perspective. Document the purpose of the project in your project charter and validate your charter with your sponsor and other key stakeholders. As part of the chartering process, discuss tolerance for risk and investigate what your key stakeholders believe may be risky about your project.

Also review your key processes with your sponsor during project initiation, especially the process for decision making and problem escalation. Set expectations for how you will be communicating requests, and for how quickly you will expect resolution. If possible, obtain approval for a process that allows you to make decisions and move forward if the sponsor is unavailable or fails to respond in a timely way.

Work with your sponsor to organize a project start-up workshop, and set time aside on your agenda for your sponsor to participate, either at the beginning or at the end of the workshop.

Planning Your Project

If your project is large or complicated, set expectations with your sponsor that will allow adequate time and effort for planning. If your project planning will take more than several days, update your sponsor at least weekly on your progress.

As you begin to wrap up your planning process, prepare a summary of your plans for discussion with your sponsor. Set up a one-on-one meeting with your sponsor and review your plans. If your plans support the initial objective for the project, validate them with your sponsor and set the project baseline. If your plans show that the project objective is inconsistent with the project's goals, develop a clear and concise summary that shows why. Discuss the project's risks with your sponsor and use your risk analysis to support a request for budget or schedule reserve. Use your data to negotiate a realistic baseline for the project and get approval from your sponsor to proceed.

Executing Your Project

Communicate frequently during the project to keep your sponsor up-to-date. Avoid needless detail in your communications, but be thorough and honest in your reporting.

When you do run into problems, communicate the project's status promptly and always include your plans for resolution. Use your escalation process only when absolutely necessary, but escalate quickly whenever you run into an issue that you are unable to resolve on your own. Throughout the project, manage changes diligently. Use your sponsor's authority to avoid changes that are not necessary.

Most of all, strive to appear competent. Whether you actually know what you're doing or not, ensure that it always seems that you do.

17. What can I do when my project loses its sponsor?

Projects always begin with a sponsor. Sometimes as a project progresses, however, sponsors move on, lose interest, or otherwise disengage from projects that they initiate. Strong sponsorship is essential for a successful project manager so if you do lose your sponsor, work to find a new one as soon as possible.

Identifying Sponsor Candidates

Any managers in your organization who will suffer consequences if your project fails are potential new sponsors for your project. Other possibilities to consider are managers who have the authority to cancel your project. The best replacement sponsor candidates will be managers who have a passion for your project's goals, or who deeply care about something that is served by the objective. If you find several potential candidates, initially consider managers who are at a level not too far above your project and within your own organization.

Selling Your Project

Before you approach a potential new sponsor, summarize your business case. Begin by developing an "elevator speech," a short description of your project that takes no more than a minute to present. In your elevator speech, stress aspects of your project that you believe will matter to the potential sponsor. Also be ready to discuss your project vision. Describe how things will be different when the project is completed, for the organization as well as for your potential sponsor.

If your potential new sponsor seems reluctant, you may be able to solicit persuasive help from your former sponsor, managers higher in the organization, or some of your key stakeholders.

Securing Sponsor Commitment

Build the best case that you're able to and request a commitment from your potential sponsor to support your project. If you are not able to get commitment, identify another candidate and try again. Keep working until you have successfully secured a replacement sponsor.

When you have found a replacement, maintain your new sponsor's support through effective ongoing communications, face-to-face meetings, and other regular interaction.

18. How can I secure and retain adequate funding throughout my project?

The most important factor in ensuring adequate funding is maintaining strong project sponsorship. As discussed in the previous two problems, strong sponsorship depends upon keeping the formal commitment of your sponsor and understanding your sponsor's perspective on "what's in it for me?"

Using the Project Business Case

Every project has two financial numbers that really matter. The larger number (at least it's assumed to be the larger number) is what the project is worth—its value. The second number is what the project costs—its budget. If the business case for the project is sound and the value is significant, then defending your project funding may only require periodic reminders of what the project is worth to your key stakeholders. When setting the project baseline, use planning and other bottom-up project analysis to justify an adequate budget. Secure a firm funding commitment for your project baseline, including sufficient reserve to deal with identified project risks. Maintaining adequate project resources begins with setting a realistic budget tied to thorough project planning.

Shielding your project from cuts also may depend on having a strong and compelling project vision that vividly illustrates both what will be better when the project is done and what adverse consequences are likely if it is not successful.

Communicating Progress

Use your weekly or other periodic status reporting to show progress against your project baseline, and to emphasize that you are on track and moving successfully toward closure. Always be prepared to quickly analyze the impact of proposed changes such as staff reduction or reduced funding. At the first rumors of cuts, prepare a summary showing the impact of the changes, in terms of schedule delays, reduced quality or other scoping changes, or increased project risk. Discuss the consequences of such changes with your sponsor and other key stakeholders, relying on plan-based data, not just vague paranoid-sounding worries.

Protecting Your Priority

Regardless of how persuasive you might be, there are times when cuts must be made in organizations. Best-in-class organizations manage such "right-sizing" (or whatever the currently favored euphemism may be) using priority analysis and portfolio management. They defer or cancel projects that are less important, and maintain funding, sometimes even increasing it, for the most critical projects. This approach, however, requires good data and a lot of effort, so many organizations use the simpler method of across-the-board cuts. If the organization needs to save 10 percent, all projects have their budgets reduced by that amount, often through staff layoffs.

Even in the face of flat reduction goals, though, priorities do matter. If your project has an attractive business case, recognition of the importance of your project may be obvious. If you are nearing project completion, enhance your priority by emphasizing any timing consequences resulting from funding or staffing reductions. For some projects, completion and delivery of results may well be a critical component in dealing with the problems that led to the cutbacks. When facing organizational resource reductions, ensure that your sponsor and stakeholders have all the justification for your project that you can provide to them. Work through them to increase the priority of your project relative to competing projects and other ongoing endeavors.

19. Can the project management function be outsourced?

Depends on:
- ▲ The relationship of the project to other work
- ▲ Whether the project relates to an organizational core competence

Avoiding Outsourced Project Management

This problem may be the easiest in the entire book; the answer to this question is almost always "no." Effective project management is so thoroughly woven into the fabric of an organization that outsourcing should be considered only as a last resort. Organizations implement their strategies through projects, so it's good practice to ensure that project managers understand and care about the business. Having project managers in charge who work for other organizations can result in potential motivation and alignment issues, and may lead to conflicts of interest and other difficulties.

Many projects are undertaken as part of ongoing and long-term organizational objectives, for which there may be important subject matter and process considerations. If project managers are not part of the permanent organizational picture, necessary competencies to support future work and new initiatives may be unavailable.

In addition to all of these considerations, very few projects are undertaken in a vacuum. Project managers responsible for related projects must communicate effectively and work together seamlessly. Project leaders who are outsiders can cause significant problems on large complex programs, and may also impede smaller project efforts where frequent interaction is necessary.

Outsourcing decisions can consume a lot of effort, but it can be dangerous and expensive to take shortcuts. Too frequently, organizations decide to outsource work based upon the answers to two overly simple questions. The first question is: "Is this project necessary?" When the answer is "yes," it's followed by the second question: "Do we have anyone available to lead the project?" Because the answer is almost always "no," the outsourcing option can be nearly inevitable. Although there are cases where outsourcing project leadership can work well, hiring

46

outsiders to run projects based only upon the answers to these two questions can be disastrous.

Adopting Outsourced Project Management in Exceptional Circumstances

There are exceptions to most rules, however, including this one. Outsourcing project management can be a very good decision in any situation where the project involves work with which no one in your organization is familiar, especially if it is unlikely to be repeated in the future. Projects to convert to new software, hardware, systems, or other new infrastructure may be most efficiently and inexpensively completed using project teams and managers who specialize in the work that is necessary. Outsourcing may well be the best solution for any one-off project that is mandatory but that has little or nothing to do with the ongoing work of the organization.

Another key consideration when thinking about outsourcing project management is the amount of project independence. If the project truly has nothing to do with other current project work, outsourcing it may be a good option. This works best when the technology involved is not considered key to any organizational strategy.

One final situation where outsourcing project management can make very good business sense is where an entire project is totally outsourced, along with all potential follow-on projects. When a part of your operation can be logically separated from other activities, hiring an outside firm to take full responsibility for it on a contract basis may be a good option. Some examples of this include ongoing support for obsolete products that remain under warranty, the production of noncritical but necessary components, or any other functions that you believe may be more efficiently handled by someone outside of your business. Again, this works best when the project work is not related to anything considered organizationally strategic and can be completely disconnected from other activities.

20. How can I ensure good project management practices during organizational process changes?

Depends on:
▲ The size of the organizational changes
▲ The source of the organizational changes

Anticipating Changes

Organization change is inevitable, and in some organizations it occurs with bewildering frequency. It helps if you can see it coming, so be on the lookout for potential reorganizations or management changes, widespread problems that someone will have to deal with (sooner or later), and anything significant that has the rumor mill buzzing. During times of organizational change, your current project management practices may be threatened, but with prudent preparation you can protect—possibly even improve—them.

Preserving Effective "As Is" Processes

If possible, involve yourself in the organizational change project and work to include useful current project management practices in the initial process documentation. As the change project's objectives come into focus, consider the relationship between project management and the overall project goals. Identify how your current project management practices support the desired changes. Also consider possible project management process improvements that could be integrated into the overall changes.

Integrating Project Management into the New "To Be" Processes

As the new processes are defined for the organizational change, identify any proposed modifications that relate to project management. If there are threats to good project management processes, work to minimize them. If the changes involve new management who appear to be hostile to good project management process, work to build support and communicate the effectiveness of what you're doing today. Use results, metrics, and success stories from well-managed projects to demonstrate the value of good project management. Build management support by documenting the benefits achieved by successfully managed projects.

As plans for changes to organizational processes come together, identify opportunities to include project management practices and deliverables in communication and training materials. If organizational changes could directly or indirectly have an adverse impact on how projects are managed, approach the people who are responsible for the changes and work to help them understand the problems that this will cause. Monitor pilot programs and provide feedback if the changes are having a negative impact on projects. Work to help adjust new processes so that they incorporate methods for project management that are at least as good as what came before.

Standardizing the New Processes

Update your documentation for current project management processes, and if possible, contribute similar content to the documentation associated with the new organizational process. If you're not able to get directly involved, at least work with the people who are responsible to ensure consistency.

If there are any changes to project management processes as part of an organizationwide change effort, explain them to your team, your sponsor, and your key stakeholders. Work to establish their support and buy-in.

21. What is the best structure for program management for ensuring satisfactory customer results?

Depends on:
▲ Overall complexity
▲ Program size

Dealing with Programs

The principles of project management work best with relatively small, straightforward undertakings. As the magnitude and complexity of the work increases, project management practices are no longer sufficient, so your success will also depend on *program* management principles.

Complexity has several dimensions. Technical complexity is related to the deliverable and the processes required by the work. Another aspect of complexity arises from the number of independent teams of people who must work together, and complexity grows significantly if any of the teams involved are from different organizations. The expected magnitude of the undertaking also matters, and whether measured by overall staffing, the budget, or the number of involved locations, size increases the number of potential failure modes. To effectively deal with all of this, program management relies heavily on the principles of decomposition and delegation. Programs are broken up into projects where the work teams can be managed independently by project leaders who have responsibility for interrelated projects small enough to be consistent with project management practices.

A number of later problems in this book will discuss program management practices related to planning and execution, but doing this well depends on setting up a program office and establishing effective communication.

Establishing a Program Office

For modest-sized programs having a small number of independent teams and manageable complexity, there may be little need for a program staff or centralized processes. As programs grow in size, however, a program office becomes a necessity. The program office for a substantial set of interrelated projects will have a potentially sizable staff. Functions that may be managed by members of a program staff include:

▲ Identifying and documenting processes to be used for the program
▲ Establishing and enforcing program policies, methods, life cycles, and review policies
▲ Providing education, training, and consulting
▲ Supporting project planning
▲ Assisting with facilitation of project meetings
▲ Establishing centralized contracting, time tracking, and financial practices

The program staff also has responsibility for overall program planning, risk management, resource analysis, and program-level reporting. The size of the program staff will scale with the size and complexity of the program, but typically it will have approximately one person for every twenty people associated with the overall program.

Communicating Effectively

Program communication requirements are very complicated. Internal communications involve inbound status sent from the project leaders, broadcast messages to the project leaders, and even more messages among the project leaders. External communications include interactions with customers, stakeholders, steering committees, and others.

Program control relies on effective and well-organized online program information storage with both adequate access for all contributors and appropriate security. It also depends on frequent, clear communication of program status information, and open two-way communication encouraged at all levels of the program hierarchy.

22. How do I effectively manage customer expectations?

Depends on:

▲ Having a known or single customer versus having a "market" customer

▲ Having users who may not be the economic buyer

Uncovering Needs and Wants

Work with your sponsor and key stakeholders at the beginning of the project to glean what they know about the customer's needs. Document what is thought to be known and work to verify your information directly with customers and users. If the customer is known, set up meetings to discuss what the project will deliver. Whenever possible, watch the customer work in the environment where your project deliverable will be used; there may be big differences between what customers will tell you and what they actually do.

Some projects engage in product development for users who are part of a market and cannot be identified in advance. If this is the case, plan to meet with past customers who are thought to be representative of the intended users for your new project's deliverable. Consult available information about your prospective customers, and when necessary, plan and execute market research among target customers to better understand the market and its requirements.

Work to validate the requirements for your deliverable. List both what the deliverable *is* and what it *is not*. The first list will include all of the requirements you have validated as mandatory for your project. A good *is not* list isn't simply a list of ridiculous things that no one would ever imagine as part of your project. It includes reasonable features and potential requirements for your deliverable that customers would probably find desirable, but that you nevertheless plan to exclude from your project.

An *is not* list can be a very powerful tool for managing customer expectations. The list of things you will not deliver sets boundaries for your project, and it provides a comprehensive basis for scoping discussions with your users and customers. Some of the things initially listed on your *is not* list will be acceptable, and discussing them will enable you to eliminate them from customer expectations. Other items listed will inevitably be unacceptable, and discussing them will provide you guidance for adjusting your project scope. Either way, documenting both what your deliverable *is* and what it *is not* will help ensure consistency in how you and your customers perceive the project scope.

Investigating Feasibility

When defining project scope, also work to determine what is possible and what is not. If you suspect that some aspect of your project deliverable is infeasible, initiate project activities to investigate. If your investigation shows that something expected by your customer is probably impossible, document why and use your data to discuss it with your stakeholders and customers to ensure that it is excluded from the scope.

As an alternative, if some aspect of your project appears excessively risky, make firm commitments only to what you realistically believe that you can deliver. It is always better for projects to underpromise and overdeliver than to do the reverse.

Documenting Scope Clearly

Customer expectations are set in the beginning of the project, but they matter most at the end. Meeting customer expectations requires that you establish and validate the evaluation and acceptance criteria early, so when they are applied at the end of the project there will be no surprises. Doing this as part of initial project scoping is effective in ensuring that you understand why each requirement in your project scope is important to your users, and how they will judge whether you have met their needs. Establishing validation criteria at the beginning of the project will also help you to eliminate any requirements that are not mandatory.

Throughout your project, manage your customers' expectations using ongoing discussions; feedback from testing; demonstration of prototypes, pilots, mock-ups, and intermediate deliverables; and other periodic customer interaction. For lengthy projects, revalidate your requirements at least every six months, using additional customer interviews or market research as necessary. Scrupulously use a well-defined change management process similar to that described in Problem 84. Work closely with your customers and stakeholders to manage expectations following any accepted change that results in significant scope modification.

23. How can I reconcile competing regional/cross-functional agendas?

Depends on:
▲ Sponsorship authority
▲ Alignment of priorities

Establishing One Version of the Truth

At the first signs of disagreement over matters that could significantly affect your project, begin to draft a single document that you can use to summarize any controversies. Start the document by listing everything generally related to the conflict (or potential conflict) where there is general agreement.

Next, identify aspects where you are aware of, or suspect that there may be, differences of opinion. Before adding anything about them to your document, consider how you would prefer to deal with each one. Ultimately it's your project, so your opinion matters a lot, and it also represents what you think will be the best route to project success. Note your preferences for each of the open issues, and then document any other perspectives that you are aware of.

Next, set up a meeting with your sponsor to discuss the situation. Outline the points of general agreement to your sponsor, and then explain the reasons for your preferences on the remaining issues. In your presentation, emphasize how your recommendations contribute to goals that you know are important to your sponsor. Sponsors can react to controversial open issues in one of three ways. The most desirable response is that they agree with you and will use their authority to intervene and resolve the conflict. A second response is that they favor your recommendation but either do not wish to get involved or lack the authority to make much difference. The third possibility is apathy—they do not have an opinion and are content to leave things up to you.

For issues where your sponsor is willing and able to intervene on your behalf, you can at least tentatively move the item into the upper portion of the document containing areas of agreement. (Even in cases where decisions can be forced using higher authority, it is always a good idea to verify that they will be accepted with minimal hard feelings. Getting your way through force and aggravating people you must work with in the process may do your project more harm than good.)

In cases where your sponsor supports your position but will not or cannot force the issue, include his or her preference on the list along with yours. In the worst case, where your sponsor declines to get involved, you will need to proceed on your own. For both of these situations, you will need to negotiate and find compromises.

Building Consensus

Identify all the stakeholders whom you want to come to agreement. To the best of your ability, list them in order of relative organizational authority. Set up a meeting with the individual with the most power and influence on your list to discuss your document. Verify agreement with the items at the beginning of your document, including any of them where your sponsor has intervened. For the other items, verify stakeholder agreement with your position for all items where you concur. For the items where you disagree, ask about priorities and motivations and probe to discover the sources of conflict. As you proceed, note your stakeholder's expressed preferences for each controversial item, adding them to your document. Without making any commitments, promise to return to discuss this further.

Schedule similar individual discussions with your other stakeholders and use what you learn with each to guide your discussions with those who remain. Get a good sense of where people agree with your recommendations and where they do not. Where there are differences, determine how much each one matters. Work to determine if any of your stakeholders might escalate any residual disagreements into project showstoppers.

For some controversial items, there may be a solid majority of the stakeholders in agreement with your recommendation. If so, poll the minority to see if they all might be willing to acquiesce. For matters where you can generate acceptance, document the majority position and move on. If there is a majority in favor of a position that you disagree with, assess how much adopting it would affect your project. If you decide that you can live with it, capitulate.

For any issues that remain, there are other tactics to try that may lead to resolution. You can meet together with the stakeholders who feel most strongly—pro and con—about an issue to see if coming together might result in agreement. Sometimes "getting all the liars in the same room" will cause opinions to shift. There may also be options beyond those already being considered, and a "third way" compromise might emerge that would be acceptable to all.

As a last resort for issues where discussion and principled negotiation fails to bring agreement, you may need to escalate to higher authority. Even if sponsors and managers initially appear indifferent, you will usually be able to engage them in dealing with matters where your project's success or failure hangs in the balance.

Documenting Agreement

Update your summary with all the items and their associated decisions. Circulate it to your sponsor and stakeholders, verify their acceptance, and use the decisions to guide your project.

24. How should I effectively deal with contributor hostility or reluctance during start-up?

Project contributors tend to be either allies or adversaries. During initiation, you will need to identify all those who are adversaries and either convert them into allies or determine how to proceed, either by doing without them or by finding a way to deal with the effects of their behavior on your project.

Determining the Need for Involvement

If someone on your project team is not supportive of the project, determine if their participation is essential. Investigate alternatives, such as using different contributors with similar skills and talents, or other methods for completing project work that could be delegated to others on your project team. On some projects it may even be possible to do without one or more of the contributors who are initially assigned to your project entirely. If you have a good alternative, adopt it, and remove unnecessary staff members who seem likely to impede your progress.

Converting Adversaries

If there are no good options other than working with someone who seems hostile to your project, find out why the person feels this way. Some people are negative because of interpersonal reasons. Others may simply be opposed to the project. If you don't know why a team member seems indifferent or antagonistic, meet with the person and discuss the situation.

If the problem is interpersonal, you may be able to resolve it by building rapport and teamwork. Establishing relationships and trust is essential to gaining the cooperation of reluctant staff members. Work to find things that you and other team members may have in common with recalcitrant contributors, such as interests, studies, hobbies, past projects, likes, dislikes, or anything at all. Identify colleagues whom you have in common, especially people for whom you share mutual respect. Involve reluctant team members in project planning and decision making, using their inputs and showing that their contributions are valued. If the problem is a poor (or nonexistent) relationship and you can improve it, your project will benefit.

You may also be able to effectively deal with cases where you have a contributor who opposes your project. Begin your discussions by discovering why your team member is against your project. Perhaps the other person really does not understand your project, or has no awareness of why it's necessary. Discussing the project can bring hostile contributors around, especially if you have a compelling vision to communicate showing why the project is important to the organization and to others. If there are aspects of your project that resonate with your team member's individual priorities, emphasize them. Even if the project as a whole fails to motivate, some aspects of it may be attractive— for example, training opportunities, visibility to management, or access to information or new technology. Connecting your project to what people care about can go a long way toward converting adversaries into productive contributors.

If you are successful in gaining the support of unenthusiastic team members, it will make the rest of your project a lot easier. If, despite your best efforts, you find that you are stuck working with someone who remains hostile, you will need to deal with it. For work delegated to a team member who is adversarial, ensure that you will have ample and frequent information about progress (or lack of progress) and effective methods for escalation if there are problems. It's also best to set up the project so that any contributors who might damage team cohesion and cooperation are as isolated from others as possible. You can be successful leading unfriendly and argumentative team members, but it's a lot of work and you must guard against having adversarial attitudes damage the morale of the whole team.

Maintaining Alliances and Seeking Alternatives

Establishing support at project initiation is necessary, but not sufficient. You must sustain the initial buy-in throughout your project using rewards, recognition, and positive feedback. Keep criticisms and negative feedback in reserve, using these only as a last resort to keep things moving. Even if you find it necessary to isolate some contributors from team interactions, you will need to invest in frequent one-on-one communication and vigilant monitoring of all delegated work.

It's also prudent to have some contingent options available in the event that relationships deteriorate enough to threaten to derail your project. Investigate potential recovery tactics such as outsourcing, proactive skill building and training for more cooperative team members, use of alternative methods and technologies, or anything else that might work.

If you can convert an adversary into an ally, that's great. Project managers need all the friends they can get. However, if you do find it necessary to complete a project where one or more key contributors have remained adversaries throughout, spend some time to reflect on how you will avoid this on your next project.

25. When is a project large enough to justify investing in a two-day project launch?

Depends on:
- ▲ Project size and complexity
- ▲ Project priority
- ▲ Cohesion of the team

Justifying a Launch Meeting

Whether it is called a project start-up workshop, a launch, a kickoff, an initiation, or something else, an early meeting involving the project contributors is a great way to get a project off to a fast start. The duration of the meeting has a lot to do with the specifics of the agenda, which often includes:

- ▲ Presentations and discussion of the overall project
- ▲ Project-planning activities
- ▲ Team building
- ▲ Delegating responsibilities and obtaining buy-in

If there has been a good deal of effective communication, most contributors know each other, and the project is not very complicated, a half-day or even shorter meeting may suffice. For more complex, larger projects, however, a productive agenda can easily run to two days or even longer. The point is to set up a start-up meeting that will save more time on the project than it uses, regardless of its length.

Sizing the Meeting Agenda

In general, a launch meeting should have a duration of approximately 1 percent of the overall projected project length. A project expected to take about 200 workdays, roughly ten work months, can easily justify a two-day start-up workshop. Shorter projects that are complicated or novel will also profit from a couple days of focused work and discussion. Another consideration for setting the length of the agenda is the relative familiarity of the people on the project team. If the team has never worked together before, the meeting will provide the initial foundation the project will depend upon for effective teamwork, and this does take time. This aspect of a project kickoff meeting is particularly important for project teams that are geographically distributed and do not expect to see much of each other during the project. One of the main objectives of an effective project launch is to build a high-performing team; without sufficient face-to-face time this will be very difficult, if not impossible.

Evaluating Trade-Offs

If obtaining approval for an in-person, multi-day project start-up meeting proves difficult, develop data estimating both the cost of holding a meeting and the cost of not doing it. While the costs of doing such a meeting—travel, logistics, hours of people time—are generally easy to assess, the costs of not conducting the meeting may be less obvious. In addition to the loss of an excellent opportunity to build teamwork, relationships, and trust, there are other substantial costs associated with not holding a project launch. The concentrated effort of a project kickoff exercise combines the high energy of the start of a new project with a tight focus on its initial planning and setup. A day spent in a project start-up workshop, particularly when conducted off-site with minimal distractions, can equal several days of effort spent in a normal work environment. Another significant opportunity cost borne when project launch activities are shortchanged is the increased risk associated with a less cohesive understanding of the project and inadequate collaborative analysis of potential problem areas.

26. How do I establish control initially when my project is huge?

Very large projects, or programs, require a hierarchy organizing them into smaller undertakings where leadership, organization, and coordination can be delegated.

Decomposing Big Projects

Project management practices work best on projects of modest size. One way to take advantage of this on large programs is to break them up into smaller undertakings. The resulting projects may be controlled and managed by project leaders responsible for portions of the work that can be well managed. Decomposing programs into projects tends to be an iterative process, because the size, complexity, and often initially incomplete definition of major undertakings make it very difficult to get right on the first try.

Program decomposition works similarly to the work breakdown process of project management, and the objective is the same—defining manageable, better understood units of work that are equivalent to a large, chaotic-looking whole. The initial process step involves logical analysis of the entire job, looking for pieces that can be separated and managed autonomously, or at least mostly autonomously. The first step is often assigned to specialists, such as architects and urban planners for construction projects, systems engineers for hardware projects, software architects for applications, or other high-level experts associated with large projects of other types.

Program decomposition has two main goals. The first goal is to establish projects that are small enough to be independently managed well by project leaders using the principles of project management. The second goal, which is equally important, is to identify all significant interconnections between the projects and to minimize their number. Control at the program level depends on delegation to project leaders who will competently manage the project work for which they are responsible, and also on identification and management of each of the interproject dependencies. When there are too many interface connections between projects within a program, it is a sign that you should go back to the drawing board and try again. A program with ten projects and 500 interproject dependencies will be unmanageable. The goal of the decomposition process is to establish a hierarchy, with multiple levels if necessary, where the component projects are sufficiently independent that the project leaders can focus primarily on the work of their teams, and where there are no more than about a dozen interfaces to track in each reporting cycle for the program.

Initiating and Planning Programs

Program control begins with identifying competent leaders for each project. Seek project managers who are experienced in the work and can make a full-time commitment to the program. Effective delegation requires buy-in and ownership, so involve all of the project leaders in program definition and planning.

Successful program and component project planning depends on clear program-level definition information. Clearly define and communicate all expected life-cycle deliverables and testing and acceptance criteria. Work with your project leaders to ensure a consistent, shared understanding of your program objectives so that the work they manage independently will remain consistent.

Program and project planning will begin in parallel. Following program decomposition and assignment of project leaders, the next step is to have the project leaders develop plans for their projects. When completed, these individual plans can be pulled together by the program manager, who works with the project leaders to find issues. The list of issues, along with any suggestions for resolution, may then be used to start a second planning iteration. Your goal is to build an integrated set of project schedules for the work through a sequence of planning iterations. Using the individual project plans, you can build an overall program plan documenting all significant interproject dependencies. The process for doing this is explored in Problem 56.

Your success, especially in very long duration programs, also depends on periodic review and adjustment of plans and objectives. Schedule "rolling wave" planning exercises at least every six months throughout any major program.

Managing Interactions and Communication

Program control also depends upon establishing a solid infrastructure for both formal and informal communications. Ensure that overall program communications are well integrated and coordinated with project communications, and establish sufficiently formal processes for program-level issue tracking, change control, and risk monitoring. Link defined project-level processes with analogous program-level processes that will allow you to detect and manage anything that could have programwide impact.

Periodic program staff meetings also contribute to control, whether held for specific activities such as program start-up or focused on presentation of overall status. Even teleconference meetings that primarily broadcast information to large, geographically separated teams can be quite effective, especially if you provide adequate opportunity for questions and feedback.

Establish centralized archiving for project information, either integrated with your program management information system or linked to it. Ensure that all who need it have continuous access to the information they need for their work, and organize it for easy access. Provide program-level status reports at least monthly, and establish two-way project and program status reviews with program staff and project leaders at least weekly. Work to detect issues that might affect the program early, and try to resolve them before they become unmanageable.

Finally, while establishing good teamwork among all of the dozens or hundreds of contributors is unlikely, program health depends on good teamwork within each of the individual teams that do work together. Encourage each project leader to maintain good relationships within his or her project team. Build teamwork among your program staff or program office. The community of project leaders is the "core team" for the program, so you also need to maintain an environment that promotes their ongoing smooth collaboration. Anything that you can do to sustain friendly cooperation throughout the program staff will contribute to overall control.

27. How should I initiate a new project with a new team, or using a new technology?

Establishing Relationships

With a new team, a project start-up workshop or launch, discussed in Problem 25, can be an excellent way to get relationships started. Also, take advantage of all face-to-face meetings and conversations to learn more about the people on your team. Spend time initially exploring and defining roles and responsibilities on your project, so everyone knows how and where he or she fits on the team. Plan and make decisions together, so that all will have contributed to setting up the project and will see the overall effort as "ours," instead of "theirs" or just "yours." Also, involve your team in making process and other decisions about how the project will be run.

Specific activities can bring the team together, whether they are related to the project such as those above or not. It can be very effective to do something fun as a team, particularly if it helps to break up a lengthy planning or kickoff meeting. If you do decide to set up an extra-curricular activity with a new team, verify that everyone will willingly participate and find it enjoyable; it will not help teamwork to take a team prone to seasickness on even a short sailing trip. Eating is one thing that everyone has in common, and it can be an excellent way to build rapport. Provide snacks at meetings, and look for other times when you and your team members can eat together. Again, involve the team members in decisions about what to eat; not everyone will like, or can even eat, everything you may enjoy.

If you detect any signs of reluctance or hesitation from some of the people you do not know well, try willing them over with some of the ideas in Problem 24.

Dealing with New Processes or Technology

Projects are all unique, and when the differences between the current project and your past experiences are significant, you need to deal with them. If you face technology challenges, discuss them with your sponsor and key stakeholders and set expectations appropriately. Learning curve issues can be significant. Overcoming them will probably require at least time, and perhaps additional funding. If training, new equipment, travel, or other investments will be needed, discuss this with your project sponsor and negotiate for appropriate funding.

Opportunities for learning may be desirable to your contributors, so use the adoption of new technology or methods to motivate your team members who are interested in improving their knowledge and skills. If some team members are resistant to adopting novel methods or uninterested in emerging technology, either mentor them to help them adjust to and accept the changes, or involve them in parts of the project that will be less affected by them.

Adopting new approaches to your work can be a great way to keep things fresh and interesting, so be on the lookout for opportunities to improve your project methods and deliver better results. It can also be a lot easier to get people excited and engaged in a new project when there are elements of innovation; few people want to do essentially the same project over and over.

28. How should I evaluate and make "make vs. buy" project decisions?

All projects face alternatives in how to approach the work. Some organizations have deeply embedded "not invented here" cultures and they tend to reinvent the wheel whenever possible. Other environments are prone to taking shortcuts, with a bias toward cobbling together solutions using off-the-shelf components even where it might compromise the deliverable. The best approach varies with the project, so a good decision process is needed. The main considerations should be cost, fitness, timing, organizational needs, and effect on the team.

Considering Costs

Cost analysis of the make vs. buy decision is often paramount in deciding which course to take. Although this might seem easy, doing it well can be quite involved. On both sides there is a tendency to underestimate, so it helps to be somewhat skeptical.

The cost of using something purchased includes the direct, out-of-pocket purchase price, but it does not necessarily end there. You may need to customize, install, or otherwise invest effort before you can use it. There may be training and learning curve considerations as well, so it is easy to misjudge the eventual cost of employing available components. Alternatively, the cost of making what you need yourself starts with purchasing any raw materials and includes the cost of all the labor to complete it. Detailed planning for these activities is not usually available when deciding whether to purchase something or make it yourself, so effort estimates tend to be based on high-level analysis (or "guesses") and can be wildly optimistic. When contrasting estimates, consider their sources and whether anyone providing data has any related or vested interests.

Considering Fitness

Fitness is usually not difficult to assess, assuming that your project is reasonably well defined. The fitness of what you can make is generally assumed to be very good, or you wouldn't be considering making it in the first place. Fitness assessment of purchased components may also be straightforward, especially if you have applicable experience from past projects. Significant variance between what you can purchase and what you need will drive the cost estimate up, perhaps even ruling out the "buy" option.

Considering Timing

Some projects are under severe time constraints, making realistic scheduling assessments a major decision criterion. As with cost, the accuracy of timing estimates depends a lot on the quality of the analysis. It is easy to underestimate the duration for building a part or component when all the planning information is embryonic. Also, while a purchased component may seem to represent essentially no time investment, additional time for customization or other work may be necessary, and shipping times for things that are not sourced locally can be substantial.

Considering Organizational Needs

Deciding whether to make or buy what you need can also have organizational impact. Things to consider outside your project include:

▲ Is the component to be purchased related to an identified core competence?
▲ Will there be a potential competitive advantage in building the part yourself?
▲ Will a bought component affect ongoing support or warranty costs?
▲ Are there long-term considerations that could have consequences for future projects (such as potential reuse and leverage of in-house development)?

Considering Your Team

Finally, routinely purchasing what you need can affect team motivation. When most of what you need is purchased or outsourced, your team members may start to fall behind in their areas of expertise. If there are few opportunities for personal development and skill building, contributors may start to disengage, and staff turnover can become a problem.

Making a Decision

When faced with a make or buy choice, assemble what you know about each of your options. If there are considerations beyond the ones mentioned here, include that data too. Line up the information for your options against your project objectives and constraints and objectively weight them based on their relative importance. Use your best judgment to select the option that best fits your project.

29. How can I quickly engage good contract workers?

Hiring outside help has become extremely common on projects. It can be an effective way to add project team members quickly, but it can also be frustrating and consume much more time than expected.

Getting Help

Project leaders are not generally hiring professionals or contract specialists. If you need to augment your project staff quickly, enlist the help of people who know what they are doing. Some possibilities for this include your legal department, the human resources department, contracting specialists in your purchasing department, outside professionals who work with temp agencies, and lots more. Depending upon your organization and your specific needs, someone should be able to help.

If you have past experience working with contract help on projects, take advantage of it. Even if you don't have direct experience, you may have peers or colleagues who do. Consider your own experiences and those of other project managers in identifying individuals or agencies that could probably meet your needs. Bringing outside staff up to speed quickly is easiest when you are able to get people with relevant prior experience.

If you are starting something new or for some reason there is little past experience to rely upon, cast a very wide net. Finding qualified help fast is easiest when you have lots of options. Consider all reasonable alternatives for publicizing your opening, including online posting services, local professional societies, and networks of your peers. It's always better to have too many resumes to look at than too few. Winnowing a large pile of choices is a lot less trouble than trying to move forward using a tiny list of unqualified candidates.

Pick a small number of promising candidates and invite them in for an interview, or at least a telephone screening. Focus your discussions on the work that the person you need to hire will do, and develop a feeling for each candidate's competence. Also discuss rates, timing, and any other constraints to ensure that the individuals you are talking to can meet your needs.

Closing the Deal

Work quickly to evaluate the candidates you've spoken with and make your choice. Even after you have located someone whom you would like to hire, there is still potential for delay. Whenever possible, take advantage of preprinted contract forms that have been approved by your organization. This not only speeds the process, it also ensures that all required legal terms and conditions are included. If the first candidate you approach suggests significant changes to the standard contract terms, quickly investigate what this might entail. Changing contract terms often involves lawyers and can take weeks, if not months. It may be more desirable to go with your second choice than to wait for a modified contract to be approved.

30. In a large project, when should I seek commitment for overall funding?

Depends on:
- ▲ The type of project
- ▲ The novelty of the technology and process to be used
- ▲ The precision required for the funding decision

Making the Business Decision

For very large projects, there is often some funding for preliminary investigation. This initial funding usually ranges from about 2 percent to 10 percent of the expected overall project budget. Going into this phase of the project, overall estimates tend to be "rough order of magnitude," in a range that can be plus or minus 50 percent. During the initial investigation, more precise information about scoping, planning, cost estimating, and other details will be developed.

You will seek formal project approval and committed funding when you have sufficient information to make the transition from initial investigation into development. Exactly when in a project timeline this is done depends a great deal on the type of project. For projects undertaken on a contract basis, preliminary investigation concludes with writing a proposal. Guidelines for creating commercial proposals recommend that the pre-bid effort be funded at a minimum of 2 percent of the anticipated bid price. For research and development projects, 5 percent of the time and funding expected for the overall project will typically be spent in investigation—more if the effort is novel, complex, or otherwise expected to be risky. Other types of projects may use 10 percent or more of the projected total funding before making a business decision to commit to the project through to completion.

Based on your feasibility investigation and planning, there may be a significant difference between realistic funding and preliminary expectations. A good business decision relies very heavily on appropriately adjusting expectations. Business funding decisions may carry the project forward as initially envisioned, cancel the effort altogether, or proceed with modifications.

Accounting for Risk

Size is a significant risk factor, so funding for very large projects should include funding for contingencies. Alternatively, project funding may be committed only phase by phase as the project proceeds. Projects that are funded one phase at a time are generally approved based on range estimates, where the low end of the range is derived from the best current overall plan and the high end is based on risk analysis.

Adjusting the Funding Commitment

Regardless of initial funding, lengthy projects will probably be modified as they proceed. Project changes are common during scheduled project reviews at life-cycle transitions, or about every three to six months. As projects progress, you learn more about them. Months into the project you will be aware of things that you could never have known at the beginning. The more you discover, the more your ability to size the project improves. Following significant changes, you will probably find it necessary to adjust funding and re-baseline your project.

31. When working with extremely limited resources, how can I get my project completed without doing it all myself?

Not every project begins with adequate resources. If you have a well-defined project but insufficient resources to get it done, you'll need to identify and secure commitments for help.

Planning the Work

The first step in getting help is finding out exactly how much trouble you're in. Based on known scope, develop a list of necessary activities and the skills required to get them done. Make a rough assessment of how much overall effort you will need from each type of contributor your project will need. Also determine your available capacity using team members already assigned to the project. Involve current contributors in your analysis, and use their help to estimate how much additional effort will be required.

Negotiating for Help

Discuss your situation with your project sponsor, and use your effort estimates to request additional staffing and justify the assignment of more people to your project. If you're unsuccessful in obtaining new resources from your sponsor, at least enlist his or her help in requesting staffing from others in your organization.

Approach managers and individuals who may be able to help you cover any area where you have insufficient staffing. Use your influence to request help, starting with people who owe you favors. When you approach people to ask for help, consider what you may be able to offer to them in return for a commitment to work on your project. Prospective team members may want to work with you if your project is important. There might be learning opportunities or other reasons why people might find your project attractive. Consider any aspect of your project that others might consider appealing.

It also helps if your project appears to be fun. Tom Sawyer managed to whitewash his fence without actually doing any work because he made it look enjoyable. People wanted to paint his fence because he convinced them that there was nothing at all that they could do that could possibly be as pleasant as painting his fence. Making your project look like fun may be a challenge, but good project managers strive to provide a congenial environment in which people can work. Humor helps, as does maintaining good relationships with everybody on the project.

When you find someone who is willing to help, secure that person's commitment and begin involving him or her in project planning and other decision making. If you've promised anything in exchange for the person's commitment, ensure that you deliver on it.

Monitor progress throughout your project. Detect and quickly deal with all performance issues. Be proactive, especially with people from whom you do not have very strong commitments. When there is a problem, discuss it with the individuals involved. Remind people of the commitments that they have made and seek their help in resolving issues. If contributors seem to be falling behind in their work, approach them for suggestions about how to catch up.

If you lose team members during your project, repeat your capacity analysis and figure out what you need to do to restore staffing to adequate levels.

Above all, diligently monitor your progress. If you start to fall behind, make the situation visible to your sponsor, your stakeholders, and anyone else who can help. At the first signs that your staffing is inadequate, seek assistance and continue looking for help until you find it.

32. How should I initiate a project that has a relatively low priority?

Not every project can be the number one priority, so most project leaders need to figure out how to get things done even though other work may take precedence. To succeed, these projects will need sufficient priority, sustained sponsorship, and a dedicated team.

Verifying Your Priority

Before assuming that your project has low priority, discuss the situation with your sponsor. Review the project's goals and work to understand the expected benefits. If the project benefits appear substantial and inadequate priority is a credible threat to these benefits, ensure that your sponsor clearly understands this.

If your project priority is lower than appropriate, propose that it be raised. Whether or not you are successful, determine which projects have higher priority than yours and which have less. Consider tactics for minimizing damage to your project from "more important" projects.

Gaining Sufficient Sponsorship

No matter what your project's relative priority is in your organization, you can succeed if you are able to sustain support from your sponsor. Verify that your priority is high among your sponsor's responsibilities and that your funding, staffing, and other needs are reliably committed for your project's expected duration. Discuss the expectations for your project with your sponsor, and ensure that you both have a consistent understanding of the consequences of failure. Repeat this discussion with key stakeholders as well, and use these meetings to confirm their support. Document your sponsor and stakeholder commitments. Be prepared to draw on these commitments to avoid potential problems and to aid in recovery from any that do occur.

If you discover that your project does not seem very important even to your own sponsor, investigate why the project is being undertaken in the first place. Perhaps what you learn will help you enlist sufficient support from others to get you going. If you are unable to generate much interest from your sponsor or others in your organization, consider proposing that your project be replaced by one with a better business case. At a minimum, plan to set a baseline for the project that is not very aggressive, and keep your eyes open for opportunities to raise its perceived value and priority.

Establishing Team Cohesion

Teamwork is essential on all projects, but it is particularly important for projects that are not especially high profile. Building a loyal team is a good place to start, so work to establish trust and solid relationships with and between all the members of your project team. Projects that succeed do so primarily because the people working on them care about what they are doing, so seek ways to enhance the connection, buy-in, and commitment of all of your contributors to your project. Some possibilities for this include potential learning and development opportunities, the vision for the project and value of the project deliverable to each of your team members, a congenial work environment and likeable people to work with, and possibly even the lowered stress of working on a project that is not high profile and will not be constantly under a management microscope. Whatever you can uncover to build a committed team will help you to get into and through your project, regardless of its apparent priority.

33. How should I organize my project management information system (PMIS) to facilitate access and avoid "too much data"?

Projects depend on an excellent communications infrastructure, and the information archive containing essential project information is an essential part of this. To ensure that people can find the information that they need when they need it, set it up to mirror your project structure, keep current data "on top," and carefully manage trade-offs between access and security.

Managing Your Structure

Many project leaders set up online information storage to reflect the way that they think about the project, and this is not necessarily a bad idea. If the project is small and most of the team members are thoroughly involved with nearly every aspect of the work, your perspective on the project is probably similar to that of your contributors. However, it may be naïve to assume that everyone knows as much about what is going on as you do if your project is larger and involves complications such as technical complexity, subteams, or geographically separated contributors.

One approach to simplifying access to project information is to set up a hierarchy of layers and folders that mirror the way your project is organized. You can use functions, roles, locations, or any other organizing principle that will help people quickly find what they are looking for. In addition to establishing an intuitive structure for lower-level information, you will also need to decide how best to store projectwide data, such as high-level plans, scoping definitions, change and issue management records, and status reporting. Establish obvious locations for information that everyone will need to access, and ensure that it will be very visible from the top of your information hierarchy. Many knowledge management systems provide list and calendar functions useful for this; you can use them to prominently display key information and navigation links on the main access panel that people see when using Web or other network access methods.

Test the effectiveness of your proposed project information hierarchy by thinking about the questions that your team will most likely need to answer. Anticipate probable inquiries and ensure that your chosen information structure will make finding the relevant data straightforward. Although this may make your information archive more difficult to set up and maintain, it is ultimately a lot less onerous than constantly having to answer questions yourself. It will also enable your team members to self-serve rather than wait for you to respond when they need information and you are not available.

Managing Data Currency

It's great advice to keep all versions of everything in your archive. This helps you to manage where you are going in light of where you have been, and provides all the data you need to uncover lessons learned at the end of your project. But while keeping everything is good practice, a profusion of similarly named files can be confusing, and it's potentially dangerous to have stale information where people might inadvertently act on it. To avoid this, consider how best to retain older data while ensuring that what people find first and most easily is up-to-date.

If version control is available in the system you are using for information archiving, take advantage of it. Set up your storage so that the files and documents that people see in their primary views in the online archive are current, and that extra steps will be required when accessing earlier versions. Some knowledge management applications make this easy, with previous versions maintained automatically in a push-down list whenever a new file with the same name is archived. If such functionality is not available, set up "archive" folders at the same level of your structure as the files containing your most current information, and diligently move older versions out of the way and into the archive folders whenever you add or update your files. Whatever you do, do not force people to decode arcane date information buried in file names in order to locate the newest versions of plans, status, requirements, scoping definitions, metrics, reports, or other project documents.

Managing Security

To keep projects on track, especially global projects, ensure that key data people need for their work on your project is available around the clock. Your project data also must be easily accessed by everyone who needs to see it, but this may not necessarily be your entire extended project team. When you are setting up an information archive, consider who needs to see what, and as you are planning your structural hierarchy, use whatever security tools you have available to ensure that your team members can read everything they need to see but can only update files, lists, and tables where they have a legitimate need. Also, consider any requirements you may have for restricting access—for example, in cases where you have external contractors who should not be able to pull information restricted by your organization. Overall, balance the trade-off between access that is easy and open to all with your requirements for guarding confidential information.

You also must prohibit inappropriate deletion of needed information from your archive. It's not uncommon for people to want to "clean up" the archive after they complete their work, or following project changes that appear to make some of the files seem unnecessary. Some people may also try to remove files containing information that they find personally embarrassing; it's best to avoid storing information such as this in the first place, but you cannot always know exactly how people might react to every project status item. For these reasons, it is a good idea to ensure that all team members can see and update (ideally with automatic version archiving) everything they need, but also that most people cannot erase any information. Reserve the authority to delete information in the archive to only yourself and perhaps a very restricted number of people on your core team. While file cleanup may sometimes be necessary, uncontrolled deletion of project files is obviously dangerous. It may not always be obvious what information is truly no longer needed, and once a file is deleted you may not be able to get it, or its prior versions, back again. You cannot afford to run the risk of permanently losing potentially critical project information.

34. How can I organize my team for maximum creativity, flexibility, and success?

Depends on:
▲ The experience of the team
▲ The size of the team

Considering Team Experience

For new teams, especially teams with a number of novice contributors, the first steps to building a high-performing team involve transitioning through the stages of "forming and storming" as quickly as possible. Collaborating as a team in brainstorming, planning, and engaging in team-building activities will help achieve the good relationships and mutual trust required to get you into "norming," where people begin to see themselves as members of a team.

Provide mentoring and guidance for less-experienced team members to assist them in quickly becoming productive contributors. Also consider development needs for the team as a whole, and focus on any training or skill building that will help you cover your responsibilities and benefit your project.

Engage the more experienced members of your team in this mentoring and training, emphasizing your appreciation for their expertise and value to the team. Set up rewards for creativity and problem solving. When dealing with members of your team who have a long history of project successes, focus discussions on what the project needs to accomplish. Leave the details of how to do the work mostly up to them; they probably know a good deal more about it than you do anyway. Ownership and responsibility for key parts of the project are key motivating factors. Encourage self-management, and trust people with experience to do what they have committed to do—at least until you have reason to believe otherwise. As Hewlett-Packard founder Bill Hewlett was fond of saying, "People do what's expected, not what's inspected."

Considering Team Size

On small teams, and even to some extent on large ones, team-building activities and rewards for creativity can be quite effective. When the project team becomes so large that the techniques of program management come into play, however, the primary responsibility for encouraging innovation and maintaining relationships and trust will need to be delegated to the leaders of each project team. Program-level structures and incentives that facilitate how things work may help, but the key success factors that are under your control are finding project leaders who are personable and competent, and working to minimize interproject dependencies within your program. Your program will be able to take best advantage of all the talents and creativity available only if each project team is set up to work independently and can be largely self-managed.

35. How can I work effectively with other project teams and leaders who have very little project management experience?

There are times where your success depends a great deal on the competency and cooperation of other project leaders. If your peers are sufficiently experienced, things are likely to go well. If they aren't, you will probably need to help them get up to speed.

Leading by Example

If you see little evidence that the project leaders you must work with are doing what they need to do, you may be able to get them on track by providing good examples. If planning information you need about their projects is missing or unclear, share your plans and provide templates and other job aids to get them started. If the processes that they are using are not working well, offer to help them by mentoring and provide good process descriptions to them. Make reference and training materials available to help improve how they are working and to build project management skills.

Criticizing other project leaders is never appreciated or effective, but a related tactic that often works is asking a lot of questions. If a dependency that you have on a related project is progressing poorly, meet with the other project leader to discuss it. Focus on specific detailed interactions and drill into the issues. Exploring project status using fact-based questions can provide a face-saving way for others to change. Once they realize what they ought to have been doing, they can shift into it without having to admit that they had no idea what they were doing. Focus questions on timing, resource, deliverable, or other factual issues, and work suggestions into the questions for how things might be improved.

Another idea that may be effective is to recognize where there is a leadership vacuum and leap into it. If overall planning is not sufficiently coherent, offering to lead a collaborative planning exercise can not only be a good way to ensure that the planning will be done well, but also a sneaky way to teach the others involved how it ought to be done.

Using Common Tools

Another way to encourage adoption of common, effective processes is to promote the use of consistent project management tools. If everyone is using the same tool for functions such as scheduling and managing project information, you can exert a lot of influence by providing guidance on structure, tool training and mentoring, and also by providing specific examples of good project artifacts produced using the shared applications. Libraries of templates and project documents can be very influential in improving the quality of your peers' project management artifacts.

Using Your Influence

Although it is often the case that people you work with are not employing adequate project management processes because they don't know how, sometimes this happens for other reasons. Some people are process phobic and prefer not to think about what they need to do much in advance. Others may just not have much aptitude for project management. If you find that you must work with other project leaders who are just not very interested in doing it well, you may be able to change their minds by selling the benefits of good project management. For this, you can use justifications similar to those listed in Problem 36. In other situations, you might be able to escalate to your sponsor or another higher-level manager to enlist his or her help in encouraging better cooperation.

However, even in cases where you are successful in persuading (or coercing) your peers into managing their projects better, they may be grumpy about it and remain difficult to work with. Also, people with little project management aptitude or who do not believe that project management principles are useful will almost inevitably revert to their old habits eventually. Whenever your progress depends upon dragging recalcitrant project leaders into line with your current project, you should also look for ways to avoid having to work with them again on some future project.

36. How can I help team members recognize the value of using project management processes?

In some organizations, project management may be considered to be largely unnecessary overhead, replaced by Nike-style "Just do it" approaches. Even in these environments, selling people on good project practices is possible, especially if you focus on things such as benefits and pain avoidance, required or strongly recommended standards, and meaningful involvement of the people you need to convince. This problem focuses on your team members, but as mentioned in Problem 35, the ideas here can be equally effective in gaining the cooperation of your sponsor and stakeholders.

Demonstrating Benefits

Project situations vary, but when contributors push back on the use of project management processes, it's usually based primarily on the fact that the processes require work. That's true, but the assumption that not employing good project management practices will therefore be less work is generally untrue. Past projects are almost always full of painful memories, especially where there has been little planning and control. Use this pain to your advantage, showing how a more orderly approach would better deal with things that have been problems in the past, such as the overtime required for rework, rushed work on activities discovered late, the stress and panic caused by inadequate information, and the enormous "late-project work bulge" needed to bring a disorganized project to closure. Surface the issues that bother your staff and show that the overall work using appropriate processes will be less, not more.

Also discuss other benefits, emphasizing aspects that do matter to your individual staff members. Project management provides a basis for better communication and control, so there will be better and clearer guidance throughout the project. Fewer problems will mean shorter and fewer meetings during the project, and everyone hates meetings, especially unnecessary meetings. Less chaos and thrash also means more credible status and knowledge of progress, and therefore a lot less meddling by your management. Smoothly executed projects are left alone, to focus on getting the work done instead of explaining, repeatedly, what has gone wrong. Any reasons for better project management you can devise that connect to benefits that are important to your contributors will be persuasive.

Conforming to Standards

Project management is increasingly being included in standards, regulations, and organizational requirements. Some types of projects have governmental regulations that mandate certain processes, and others must adopt them either for industry compliance reasons or to remain competitive. If any of this is true for your project, point out to your team members that in addition to project management practices being a good idea there will also be significant consequences if you fail to adopt them.

Even if there are no external standards or regulations available to help you enlist cooperation, there may be organizational requirements you can cite. Project management or program management offices often set up mandatory processes, and may also provide "process police" who monitor what is going on and can help you ensure appropriate adoption. Although practices adopted to comply with prevailing rules are easily implemented, they may or may not always be entirely appropriate. Exploit any help this provides, but also monitor your results and consider alternatives if you find that obligatory processes are ineffective. Over time, use your post-project lessons learned, discussions with your sponsor and other management, and work with your peers to adjust your mandated processes so that they will be a good fit for your environment.

Customizing the Process

It is always better to have people adopt practices that they have thought of (or believe that they have thought of) than to demand that they do so "because I said you have to." Involve your team members in fine-tuning how you plan to proceed, and listen to their feedback. If there are major objections to processes you are recommending, ask those who are complaining for their alternatives. If they come up with options that appear better, consider them. If there are no better options voiced, ask if your critics would at least try things your way for a while to see how it goes.

Asking questions to guide the discussion can also be effective in convincing people that your preferred processes are desirable. Help people see for themselves how good project management practices can address and resolve their problems.

Success stories can also be compelling. Identify similar projects that have succeeded using practices you would like to adopt, and build the case for emulating what they have done.

If you encounter so much resistance that you find it necessary to begin the project without much cooperation, consider a stealth approach. At a minimum, do a rudimentary plan yourself, and use it to provide guidance to your team and track its work. In situations where things begin to deteriorate, use the opportunity to revisit the processes in use and do what you can to improve them as you proceed.

37. How do I keep people focused without hurting morale?

It is easy to keep up morale when things are going well. Projects being projects, though, this is rarely the case for long. Sustaining motivation depends on maintaining relationships, positive attitudes, recognition, and awareness of why the project matters.

Maintaining Relationships

Sustaining good relationships and trust is a recurring theme throughout this book. This is particularly important whenever a project goes through a bumpy period. If there are problems and people need to spend extra time to recover, stress and tempers tend to rise. An effective project leader works very hard to keep people focused on the situation and the work required for recovery. It does little good to "blamestorm" and waste time and energy identifying scapegoats. When everyone sees others on the team as part of the solution, faster recovery and actual progress will result, and cooperation will remain high. Although this may seem easier said than done, minimizing strife and conflict is key to surviving difficult projects.

Staying Positive

Henry Ford said, "Whether you think that you can or that you can't, you are usually right." A good part of any successful project is holding on to the belief that you will get through it. A team that believes it will fail, or even admits to significant doubts, will find this to be self-fulfilling. Good project leaders manage to stay cheerful throughout a project, and they use their positive attitude to keep everyone else moving forward with sufficient confidence. Taking it for granted that there is a solution for every problem always increases the likelihood that you will actually find one.

Keeping a positive attitude is not about ignoring problems and risks; it is the exact opposite. Effective project leaders diligently monitor for potential problems and early signs of trouble, and deal with them proactively. Looking for problems allows you to find and solve them while they are small. If you wait until they are so big that they are obvious to all, they may be too enormous to resolve.

Recognizing Accomplishments

No matter what is going on with a project, there are always accomplishments. It's always appreciated when you identify them and make them visible in your status reporting and other communications. Adding your personal "thanks" to the contributor or team members involved will help keep people engaged. In times of stress it may be hard to remember to do this, but that's when it will make the biggest difference.

Reminding People Why We're Here

Ensuring that your team members all keep a firm grasp on project objectives that matter to them personally will assist in maintaining focus, especially when you are under pressure. The work itself, the experiences gained, the skills acquired, the value of what the project will deliver, or whatever it may be that those working on the project care about will remain important to them. Reminding your staff why they did—and still do—care about the project will help keep things moving.

38. How can I involve my team in project management activities without increasing overhead?

Part of the answer to this question is that some people on the project may not need to be as involved with every part of project management as others may need to be. Some project contributors are part of your "core team" and need heavy involvement. Others are more peripheral and can be less involved; if you insist on holding all team members captive while fleshing out every detail of definition and planning, you will increase your overhead unnecessarily (and also mightily aggravate some of your team members). However, all should be involved sufficiently, and there are ways to make things easier and more efficient.

Simplifying Your Process

Project planning requires meetings, so as you are setting them up, determine your specific objectives for each proposed session in some detail. Know why you are investing in each activity, and be brutal in eliminating meetings and process steps that you don't really need. For each meeting that proves necessary, determine who should participate. For some work, such as a project start-up workshop, all will be needed. For others, a subset will be sufficient. Your team members who do not participate can provide their input and feedback afterward.

Craft an agenda for each meeting including specific outcomes and timings. Make your meetings as short as practical, and consider ways to make them more productive by improving the processes, encouraging prework, and when it appears that it could be useful, enlisting help from someone outside the project to assist in facilitation.

If you are planning meetings for subteams, don't assume that you always need to attend. There may be aspects of project planning and scoping analysis where your presence may not be needed, and might even slow things down.

Increasing Efficiency

One way to get more done with fewer meetings is to replace routine meetings on your project calendar with specialized meetings. The time is probably already scheduled, and if it can be used more effectively for an alternative dedicated purpose, take advantage of it. If the routine meeting has a few essential agenda items, retain only those and deal with them quickly so you can focus on higher-priority matters.

You may also be able to merge sessions that are focused on learning and development with project planning. If some (or all) of your team requires training in project management, integrating planning activities for the current project into the training as skill-building exercises may save a great deal of time and provide a setting for more effective planning.

Managing Reviews and Communication

As noted, it may not be essential to get everyone directly involved in creating every project artifact. For some documents, you may be able to do the initial work yourself. For others, you may be able to get things started with just a small team of contributors. If there are project staff members who are not involved with the creation of the documents, though, ensure that they are able to review and critique them. A "RACI" matrix is an effective technique for keeping track of who needs to participate in each step of the processes. The matrix assigns one of the roles to each member of your team (including stakeholders where appropriate):

- ▲ Responsible (participates in development)
- ▲ Accountable (owns the development—one and only one person)
- ▲ Consulted (reviews and provides feedback)
- ▲ Informed (is provided information but feedback is optional)

For major project management deliverables, you are likely to be the "A," with the rest of your team split between the "R" and "C" roles. "I" is a bit too uninvolved for most project management activities, so use this designation with care. Do follow up with anyone on your team who has a "C" role to ensure that each has read and understands the information distributed.

Maintaining Efficiency

Overhead matters throughout your project, too, so consider ways to lower overhead as your project progresses. Use online repositories and attachments to circulate information, and devote meeting time to ensuring that people have reviewed the materials and answering questions. Collect information using pre-populated forms, documents, or spreadsheets to save people from having to write time-consuming and complicated status summaries. Develop check forms or online surveys for collecting simple information to speed things up. Cancel unneeded meetings, and end all meetings on time or early.

39. How can I manage and build teamwork on a project team that includes geographically remote contributors?

Increasingly today, your project team is likely to be scattered far and wide. Establishing the trust and camaraderie that a high-performing team depends upon is most difficult when people are not located together, but there are things you can do to help through team building, maintaining good relationships, and avoiding favoritism.

Establishing Relationships

Nothing works better for team building than coming face-to-face, so if at all possible find a way to bring people physically together, at least briefly near the beginning of each project. The most common justification used to do this is a project start-up or launch meeting, as discussed in Problem 25. There may be other opportunities to gather your team in one place, too, so watch for them. If you are unable to gather everyone, at a minimum bring subsets of the people who will work on your project together, and travel to join them. If all else fails, find a way to meet one-on-one with every contributor assigned to your project (or at least as many as you can).

Strive to establish linkages between your team members, building on common interests, educational backgrounds, common acquaintances—anything that helps the folks you are working with see each other as colleagues and friends. Share pictures of each other, ideally taken in recreational or other informal settings that will show that this is not just about the job at hand. In this digital age exchanging photographs is easy, and posting them on project Web sites or prominently within your project management information system will reinforce that everyone is human and that you are all in this together.

It is especially important to motivate geographically distant contributors and to connect them to your project. Work to discover something about the project that matters to your remote team members, such as

95

the type of work they prefer, aspects of the project that are personally important, or anything else that can increase their motivation and buy-in. Above all, reinforce things that you all have in common, and strive to break down barriers and minimize any differences.

Maintaining Relationships

Establishing good teamwork is hard, and sustaining it can be even harder. As projects proceed, problems arise, stress builds, and conflicts are nearly inevitable. Your job as a project leader is to ensure that the first response to a bump in the road will be an effort to resolve and move past it, not the initiation of protracted battles over who caused it or e-mail flame wars that will leave everyone fuming.

Maintaining good teamwork and effective communications among distant team members is discussed in more detail in Problem 71. Focus at least as much attention on communicating with remote contributors as you do with those nearby, and work to keep the peace inside your team, dealing with potential conflicts and differences quickly and proactively.

Avoiding Favoritism

Unless all of your team is distributed, another challenge you will face is the potential for real (or perceived) preferential treatment for people who are nearby. You may never be able to completely remove all appearances of favoritism, because there are likely to be a lot more chances to interact and communicate—both formally and informally—with people with whom you are co-located. Nevertheless, you can mitigate this by communicating diligently and regularly with distant contributors, ensuring that all rewards and recognition are fair and available to all, and that responsibilities are delegated evenly. It is also good practice to ask questions to draw people out and encourage participation by everyone in teleconferences, especially for those who are not physically present and do not participate as much as those who are in the same room.

40. How do I secure team buy-in on global projects?

Support across a global team will inevitably be somewhat uneven, because the more diverse a group is, the more perspectives tend to differ. Getting buy-in depends a good deal on your investment in building teamwork, as covered in Problem 39. It also depends on the project itself, sponsorship, and "what's in it for me?"

Promoting Your Project

You may need to do some selling to gain support for your project from your stakeholders and contributors. Consider the overall business justification, and test whether there are any aspects of it that the people whom you need to have on your side particularly care about. Also develop a vision associated with the expected results of your project, and evaluate how each person you interact with could personally benefit from its successful completion. With a global project, some of this may require investigation and discussion, both with your key stakeholders and possibly with others who can help you to better understand where people are coming from. If you are successful in connecting the interests of the people you need to influence to the overall objectives of your project, you should be able to enlist their support.

If there are people who initially do not support your project, you may be able to change their minds using some of the tactics for dealing with adversaries explored in Problem 24. If, despite your best efforts, some of your stakeholders remain hostile to your project, you will need to do your best to minimize the potential damage that this could cause.

Leveraging Sponsorship

Global projects are often sponsored by upper-level managers in the organization who have a good deal of clout. If you detect a lack of support from any of the stakeholders you are depending upon, approach your sponsor and discuss the situation. Your sponsor may be willing and able to participate in project meetings. Having your sponsor's position power on your side may succeed in securing the buy-in you need. Sometimes simply reminding others of who your sponsor is will be sufficient to transform people from ambivalent to supportive; an influential sponsor's interest in your project can be very persuasive.

Upper-level managers are more likely to travel than others in the organization, so be alert for travel plans that involve sites where you seek better support. Having your sponsor drop by, even briefly, to mention the importance of your project to a reluctant stakeholder can be extremely effective in increasing his or her support.

Reciprocating with Others

Even if it is a highly visible, enterprisewide effort, your project will never be the only thing competing for people's attention. To gain the support you need, you will almost always need to provide some reasons for others to cooperate. "Giving and getting" are the basis for most human interactions, and modern projects are no exception. Consider what you might have to offer in exchange for the support that you seek. Sometimes it might be the attention and recognition associated with your project. Other times it could be a favor you have done in the past or propose to do in the future. There are many possibilities for exchange, and you are likely to find one or more plausible options for each of your stakeholders from whom you need to obtain buy-in. Be creative and flexible in developing ideas, and be sure to follow up and deliver on anything that you have promised in exchange for each person's support.

41. How can I best manage project contributors who are contract staff?

Team members who work for your organization may have many good reasons to care about your project. Contract staff, on the other hand, have less "skin in the game," and may not care much at all; they are generally not involved for the long term, and may have little in common with the rest of your team. They may not have much interest in the work because their primary connection to the project is monetary. Good project leaders work to ensure that all contributors have reasons to care about the project, including those who work for other organizations.

Establishing Relationships

Building relationships with contract employees may present some special challenges, but they need not be insurmountable. Improving teamwork starts with developing trust and a friendly working relationship. Begin, as with any contributor, with conversation to get to know one another. Seek things that you have in common, such as interests, education, past project work, or really anything. Ask outside contributors about recent accomplishments and what they are particularly pleased about or proud of. Discuss aspects of your project that are similar to what they have enjoyed in the past, and seek ways to get them involved in work on your project that they are likely to want to participate in. Ask other questions to discover what motivates them and consider how these factors could benefit your current project.

Making It About More Than Money

Involve your outsourced staff with your other team members in meetings, planning, and other project activities. Except where your organizational policies prohibit it, also include them in team building and other events as well. If there are rules requiring that outsiders be excluded from planned events, consider modifying what you have set up so you can include everyone. (If there is no way to involve everyone, you might even be better off cancelling such events.) The more you are able to encourage team interaction, the more likely it will be that you will have a high-performing team.

"Giving and getting" apply to outside contributors, too, so consider what you or your project has to offer that your contract team members would find valuable. One of the most obvious possibilities is the prospect of a continued relationship following the project, through either an extension of the contract work into future projects, or even the possibility of permanent employment with your organization. Your project could also represent a valuable business reference, which (assuming it goes well) could be instrumental in obtaining future contract work. Your project may also represent learning opportunities, or a chance to work on something new or especially interesting, or it could have other aspects that could be motivating.

Rewards and recognition are also important. The mechanisms may be different from those available to people within your organization, but there are generally at least some options. No matter what, you can at least express your personal appreciation and thanks for a job well done, and mention significant accomplishments in your status reports and other communications. You can document and send complimentary information to those who directly manage your outside contributors, and you may also find opportunities to recommend them for specific rewards available within their own organizations. Anything that successfully pulls your outside contributors closer to you and your project can work to your advantage.

Managing Contract Staff

Finally, you should read and thoroughly understand the terms and conditions of all relevant contracts. Do your best to meet all the requirements that are yours, and ensure that all invoices are reviewed promptly and paid as appropriate. If there are provisions for incentives and penalties in the contract, work to realize the benefits associated with the incentives, and make sure they are paid. Keep situations that might result in penalties visible, and strive to avoid them. Contract penalty terms may be necessary in the contract, but whatever they are they can never fully compensate for the damage to your project from the event that triggers them.

Be an effective liaison with the other party, and provide frequent feedback on the progress of your work. Detect and deal with all issues quickly, and work within the terms of the contract to ensure that your project receives everything the contract guarantees.

42. How do I cope with part-time team members with conflicting assignments?

In a perfect world, all projects would be staffed with dedicated, full-time contributors who have no other responsibilities. In the real world, we all have many demands on our time, and at least some of the contributors on typical projects will also be committed to other projects. Succeeding in this environment depends on realistic and meaningful commitments, adequate involvement, and support from other managers.

Getting Commitments

Particularly with part-time contributors, relative priorities are a prime consideration. Ask your team members who have significant other demands on their time about priorities for your project and their other work. Also inquire about their perception of both the importance and the urgency of the other work relative to your project. If your overall impression is that you will have to struggle to get their attention when you need it, you might consider investigating more reliable staffing alternatives. Before that, however, explore any concerns that you have with the individuals' managers to verify what you are hearing. If you remain concerned about particular part-time contributors, discuss options with your sponsor for adjusting overall priorities in favor of your project, or potential alternatives for proceeding that minimize your dependence on them.

Even if you do have reasonable confidence in your staffing, verify exactly what "part time" means. If the commitment is for half time, how many hours per week will that represent? Will it vary from week to week? If the commitment is less than 20 percent, will it represent a meaningful contribution? (Meetings and other communications could use that much time, and leave little or none for other activities.) Get a good sense of when and how much time your project can expect from each person, and plan accordingly.

Involving Part-Time Contributors

As with any member of your team, involving part-timers begins with building good relationships and trust. Ask about work preferences and expertise, and get them involved with activities that they are good at, and, ideally, that they want to do. Involve them whenever possible in your start-up workshops and planning activities, and ensure that each person has an adequate opportunity at least to review and provide feedback on project documents. Ask people to provide initial estimates and other analysis for their assigned project activities, and give them ample opportunity to provide their inputs to the planning for any work they will contribute to. Uncover aspects of the project or other things you could reasonably offer that could increase their motivation and dedication to the project. Plan to take full advantage of any relevant rewards and recognition available, including frequent use of unanticipated "thank-yous." Random positive reinforcement is important for all team members, but it's particularly effective with people who are only loosely connected to your project.

Securing Other Managers' Support

As your planning nears completion, formally secure reliable commitments from both the individuals involved in your project and their managers. Communicate frequently with the managers of all of your part-time contributors, providing them with both overall project status and feedback on the work done by their people. Strive to keep things positive, and pass along as much good news as you can; when contributors realize you are on their side, they are usually more than willing to do anything reasonable you request. If you do encounter performance problems with any of your part-timers, first approach the individuals to discuss the situation and work with them to resolve the issues one-on-one, using some of the ideas in Problem 43. If you are unable to resolve matters quickly, let them know that you plan to escalate to their managers. If the problems persist, don't hesitate to escalate.

Getting and keeping meaningful part-time commitments may also involve a bit of wheeling and dealing with these managers. Explore what about your project potentially matters to the managers of your part-time staff, or if there might be something else that you can offer to them. Use what you learn to secure reliable resource commitments to your project.

43. How do I handle undependable contributors who impede project progress?

Even on relatively trouble-free projects, some tasks will be late. When the cause of the delay is (or appears to be) one of your team members, you need to confront the situation promptly and work to get the project back on track.

Verifying the Commitment and Status

When assessing project status, identify any timing problems by comparing the collected data with your baseline project plan. If you find that something has slipped, especially if the delay is likely to result in significant project problems, investigate and find out why. If the apparent cause is a failure of one of your contributors to complete an assigned task on time, meet one-on-one to discuss the situation. Start your discussion by outlining the consequences of the slippage to the overall project and any other impact it will have, emphasizing any issues that are particularly important to your individual team member.

In your discussion, verify that the initial timing commitment was clear. If it was not, determine how to ensure that any remaining due dates are well understood. If the timing commitment was clear but missed anyway, probe to find out why.

Resolving the Problem

Whether the missed deadline was clear originally or not, you'll need to work together on recovery. In determining how to proceed, work to understand the reasons for the delay. If ownership was unclear, upgrade your communications to improve on them. If your contributor lacks the knowledge, skill, or aptitude to complete the work, consider training opportunities or enlisting help from others. If there is more work to do than can reasonably be accomplished, revisit your plans either to spread the effort more realistically or to consider project changes. If higher-priority work is getting in the way, consider escalation.

Based on the root cause (or causes), consider together what the most effective approach will be for getting the project back on track. It's best to begin this dialog by asking your contributor for recovery ideas before supplying your own. If after considering your contributor's ideas you have additional thoughts, offer your own suggestions. Whenever practical, though, favor the course of action your staff member recommends; you can have more confidence in successful resolution if the recovery plans don't appear to be "marching orders" from you.

Getting Back on Track

Select a path forward that makes sense to both of you. Ask for agreement, and get your contributor's renewed commitment to follow through. Express your thanks and show that you are confident this will be successful.

In your next status cycle, verify that the project is back on track, or at least recovering as planned. If it is, remember to thank the individual and recognize the effort this required.

If the problem persists, though, confront the individual again. If working together appears ineffective, cast a wider net within your project team for recovery ideas. If all else fails, escalate to your sponsor and begin exploring other alternatives such as finding and engaging replacement staff.

44. How should I manage informal communications and "management by wandering around" on a virtual, geographically distributed team?

Informal communications with distant contributors can be a challenge, and it is more complicated than with nearby team members who are close enough to wander over and speak with. It requires planning and discipline to do well but yields substantial benefits.

Combining Formal and Informal Interactions

Your routine formal communications with remote contributors—team meetings, one-on-one telephone calls, and other periodic interactions— offer a number of openings for effective informal communications. Use small amounts of time at the start or end of team meetings to invite people to share a little about what they are up to, to reinforce that we all have a life outside of the project. A short digression about a recent sporting event involving one of the locations where you have contributors, a new film, unusual weather affecting some of your team, or some other topic of interest can be an effective use of a few minutes, especially if everyone is not yet present or dialed in. Keeping to a disciplined agenda is necessary for efficiency, but minor excursions into more personal matters need not interfere with this.

Planned one-on-one meetings at least once a week with distant staff members can also be good opportunities for side conversations on non-project issues of mutual interest. Again, start or end your planned conversations by asking how your remote contributors are doing or feeling, and if they have previously shared news of an outside activity they are involved in, express interest by asking about it.

Other Interactions

Travel when you can to visit distant contributors, and do what you can to enable your team members to travel to you on a regular basis. Coming face-to-face at least twice a year is very helpful in maintaining good relationships, and ensures that the use of telecommunications and other distance-spanning technologies remains as effective as possible between visits.

When you schedule reviews, celebrations, or other special meetings, plan to involve your remote team members, or set up parallel events that they can participate in so no one is excluded or marginalized.

Practicing "Tele-MBWA"

Informal communication is mostly about unplanned interactions, and one tactic for this on geographically distributed teams is to practice "tele-MBWA." Management by wandering around, or MBWA, is a technique popularized by Bill Hewlett and Dave Packard in the days shortly after they founded the Hewlett-Packard Company. MBWA is based on unscheduled conversations that are not centered on business matters. Particularly when HP was small, both founders strove to forge personal relationships with everyone in the fledgling company. As the company grew, this philosophy remained important; both founders were always known as "Bill and Dave," even well after their retirements. All managers at HP were encouraged to practice MBWA, *especially* those for whom it did not come very naturally. Using communications tools to practice MBWA with those who are not nearby is a variant on this tried-and-true method for building trust and relationships.

The key to MBWA, whether with team members who are close by or far away, is to do it fairly frequently, at least several times a month. It's also important that MBWA be spontaneous and without any agenda. If necessary, schedule the time required to be spontaneous—add time to your calendar at random intervals to protect the time for yourself and to serve as a reminder, and consult the schedules of others to ensure that they are likely to be available and open to a conversation. Pick times that are convenient to your remote team members, even if they are not convenient to you. Be considerate of the other people's time by doing it near the start or end of their day or near a mealtime or other break to avoid fragmenting their productive work time. Be a good listener, and never restrict or try to steer these conversations. Let the other person do most of the talking. Ask open-ended questions, such as, "Are you happy here? Do you like your job? What would make it more meaningful and productive? How is your family? How was your vacation?" Whatever you hear, don't argue. The main point is to get to know the people you are working with and to demonstrate that you care about them as individuals, not as some sort of interchangeable automatons assigned to your project. You are establishing an open environment of trust and working to really get to know your project staff.

Make these frequent spontaneous phone calls, even if you're not terribly comfortable doing this at first; it becomes easier with time and practice. Do this often enough to stay in touch, but back off your frequency if it appears that people find the conversations intrusive or annoying. Include all of the team in your MBWA, both those at your location and all who are at a distance, and try to do it evenhandedly, not just focusing on your team members who are nearby, are easy to talk with, or share your interests. This kind of informal communication is not a waste of your time because in times of stress and difficulty—and all projects have them—prompt and effective recovery depends on the relationships and teamwork you have established. Personal involvement is always essential to good project management.

45. When should I delegate down? Delegate up?

Project management, unless you plan to do all the work entirely by yourself, involves a good deal of delegating. We delegate to ensure ownership and coverage for all the work necessary, and also to gain confidence that the applied resources will be adequate to complete the project. Delegate project work to your team to align your tasks with the people who are in the best (or at least an adequate) position to get it done. Delegating work upward can be a bit tricky, but you'll need to do it whenever you lack authority to proceed or you need coverage for responsibilities that cannot be provided within your team.

Delegating Down

Delegation is a basic foundation of project planning. The work breakdown process decomposes a whole project into smaller pieces, both for better understanding and to ensure that each part can be assigned to a single person who will accept ownership and be responsible for its completion. In delegating project activities to your team members, you are assigning ownership of a portion of the overall project to each contributor. Ownership, when accepted voluntarily, enhances buy-in to the project objective, builds teamwork, and increases motivation.

Delegate responsibility for all tasks in your project downward to your team members. Align the work with contributors who are competent and willing to accept the responsibility, involving them in the definition, estimation, analysis, tracking, and all other aspects of the specific tasks. Effective project leaders delegate nearly all the defined project activities. Project management is a full-time job, so it is risky to retain ownership of too many scheduled project activities yourself. Seek named owners other than yourself for all project tasks, even if you suspect that you will ultimately have to assist in bringing some of them to closure.

Successful projects require more work than just the planned activities. There are also a wide range of responsibilities related to project management processes to account for, most of which are probably yours. Normally, you will do most of the communications and reporting for your project, lead most of the meetings, and do other things that serve as the "glue" to hold your project together. That said, there can be situations where you may want to delegate some of this to others. If you have a distributed team, it could make sense to delegate some organizational tasks. If there are technical complexities beyond your understanding, you may need to delegate parts of the project definition and documentation to appropriate subject matter experts. For very large projects that are managed as programs, you will undoubtedly find it necessary to delegate management activities to the individual leaders of the component projects, as well as to any program staff members that you have on staff. In general, though, you should always delegate the "nuts and bolts" of project management somewhat reluctantly. It's your project, and the more you delegate fundamental project management responsibilities to others, the less control you will have.

Delegating Up (or to Peers)

The most obvious cases where project leaders delegate upward involve situations where they lack sufficient authority to proceed. Decisions involving significant amounts of money, life-cycle review approvals, or other aspects of project work beyond your control are often "kicked upstairs." Escalations of problems you are unable to resolve at your level of the organization are other frequent examples. To delegate upward as smoothly as possible in these situations, create a presentation or prepare a document that clearly summarizes the facts at hand, sets a clear deadline for resolution, and provides your thoughts or recommendations on the matter. When you do have to delegate work upward, strive to appear as competent and professional as possible, and do it only when it is really necessary.

With time-sensitive decisions and approvals, emphasize why a prompt response is needed and clearly explain any consequences of delay. Consider advising your sponsor or manager that the pending response is essential to your project and that you plan to include its status in your next status report assigned to that person by name. Threatening your management with a potential "red stoplight" indicator can be very effective in generating a timely response. The downside is that if it is late, you'll need to follow through, which may not be appreciated. (And if you don't follow through, the next time a similar situation arises you'll be ignored.)

When you are asked (or told) to do something significant that diverts your time and attention away from your project, you will need to delegate some of your responsibilities. You will also, sooner or later, take some time off from work—even project leaders get to take at least a little vacation. Many of your responsibilities can probably be handled adequately by someone on your project team, so plan to cover as much as possible that way. (This is a good way to further involve your contributors and increase their buy-in, and it's also useful in finding out if some of them might make effective project leaders.) There are usually a few things, though, that you cannot delegate downward.

One option is to enlist the help of a peer, generally by committing to cover similarly in the future for him or her in exchange. Another option is to get your manager or sponsor to cover for you. This can be a good alternative in cases where your management is responsible for the situation taking you away from your project in the first place. If you are asked to travel for business reasons unrelated to your project (such as for a meeting with a potential client or to a customer hot site), prepare a list of things that require attention in your absence and assign them to the manager who is sending you on the trip. (If your list appears sufficiently burdensome, perhaps the travel request will be passed along to someone else.)

Even when you successfully delegate work to those above you in the organization, it's ultimately still your project. When requesting help, provide as much guidance as necessary to ensure that things will continue smoothly in your absence before you disappear, and be prepared for at least a little cleanup when you are able to reengage.

46. How can I best deal with project teams larger than twenty?

Very large projects are most successfully treated as programs, a collection of related but largely autonomous projects responsible for bits and pieces of the overall objective. Even more than on smaller projects, a program will benefit organizationally from a start-up or launch meeting, as described in Problem 25. Establishing a program team infrastructure is also essential, as discussed in Problem 26. This problem focuses on the structural hierarchy, communications, and team interactions useful in running a complex program.

Establishing a Program Hierarchy

Program management uses a hierarchy of interrelated projects to minimize and control the complexity, assigning the required large number of contributors to one project or another as necessary. The "core program team" is made up of the program manager, the leaders of the various projects, and any members of a program staff directly reporting to the program manager. In one program that I worked on at Hewlett-Packard, there were about 200 contributors at any given time, working on more than a dozen separate subprojects. In addition, we had a small program staff of about a half-dozen people who reported to the program manager (who was an IT director), which included me. My role was program planner, and I was responsible for the overall program plans, for the detailed plans supporting each of our quarterly releases, and for coordinating the contents and status of all of the detail-level project plans. Most of the contributors did not report directly to the program manager, but we were able to establish a strong matrix for the program early on that treated the managers who were responsible for all the necessary functions and individuals as de facto members of the program staff.

Throughout the program, this core program team varied in size but was generally approximately fourteen people. All of the members of this team appeared on program organization charts, were tightly involved in all planning and tracking, and attended weekly program staff meetings. No distinction was made on the program team based on management reporting relationships, and we put a lot of effort into ensuring that the primary loyalty for each team member was to the program, rather than elsewhere.

As with this program, the appropriate control structure that emerges for your program will mirror the decomposition of your work into projects, along with any necessary program staff needed to ensure that all responsibilities are well covered.

Communicating in Layers

Communication is important on any project; on large, complex programs either you communicate well or you deal with constant chaos and disaster. Layered communication is one effective way to provide people with information they need without overwhelming them with too many data.

Both for those inside the program and for external stakeholders, you should maintain a program Web site or similar place for storage of general high-level information on the program, with pointers to more detailed and more specialized information stored elsewhere online.

For those working on the program, "all hands" conference calls roughly once a month can serve as a "virtual" program team meeting. The main part of these mass meetings will generally be presentations created in advance by the program manager and staff members (typically two or three people each month). This part of the meeting would be roughly forty minutes of a one-hour scheduled conference call, and the supporting presentation materials are posted online and distributed in advance to all program contributors. The remaining time on the agenda should be reserved for questions and general interactions. For global programs, keep everybody synchronized by holding the meetings more than once. The HP program I helped manage scheduled two conference calls monthly, ten hours apart on the same day, to accommodate participants worldwide.

More frequent and detailed meetings and e-mails are used to focus on specific portions of the program. For this HP program, the weekly program staff meetings, weekly release meetings, and other weekly project status meetings all covered details relevant to the participants. Meeting summaries were sent to distribution lists set up for each to ensure that all involved had the current information needed for their work. The published reports and meeting minutes served as the definitive source for up-to-date program information.

Archiving Information

In addition to distributing weekly status and other current information to the program contributors on our large IT program, we posted all the detailed information for reference to our knowledge management system. Our online knowledge management system provided all program team members with around-the-clock access to the current status as well as all earlier versions. The archive we set up was very effective, and generally in line with the advice in Problem 33. Specific content areas we established included:

▲ **The Program Plan of Record.** The plan of record (POR) was a high-level document that was maintained in a partitioned workspace where all could read it, but only a small number of people on the program staff could update it.

▲ **Overall Program Information.** We maintained general program-level information in a number of folders set up for program plans, interconnections between the separately managed projects, information specific to each release, program staff information, and other matters of interest across the program.

▲ **Program Function Details.** In addition to general program folders, we also had sections for each functional area and geographic region, where team-specific information could be centrally maintained and made available to all.

▲ **Change Requests and Status.** All change requests were centrally stored and used to track the many hundreds submitted over the course of the program, and used for scoping future program releases.

▲ **Process Documentation.** We also centrally maintained all key program process descriptions in the knowledge management system.

▲ **Program Lessons Learned.** At the end of every release (sometimes more frequently when things were particularly bumpy), we conducted a retrospective analysis. We identified the top three areas of improvement and took action on them each cycle. We also archived all our retrospective survey information for later reference.

In setting up a program management information system, organize it from the perspective of the program team members. Make it as easy as possible for contributors to find the information they need.

47. What can I do to manage my schedule when my project WBS becomes huge?

Depends on:
- ▲ Project novelty
- ▲ Experience of your team

Breaking Up Big Projects

"Huge" is a relative term. When project activities follow general guidelines of being roughly eighty hours of effort or two to twenty workdays in duration, it's generally agreed that project management principles can easily deal with up to about 200 of them. For projects that are blazing trails into unknown territory, or working with very large teams to aggressively compress a project timeline, the total number of activities is substantially less; the tasks of coordination and communication can overwhelm the project leader at 100 total activities or even fewer. If the project is routine the number can safely go above 200, but if you stretch the limit beyond approximately 300 separate activities, things will start falling through the cracks and you will lose control.

Dealing effectively with projects that exceed these limits is the province of program management. Program management decomposes large projects into a set of separate smaller projects, each of which can be managed well using project management principles. Some programs are made up of multiple projects running in parallel, each led by a designated project leader. Other programs are set up as a series of projects, run sequentially or overlapping somewhat in time, but each having a moderate duration no longer than approximately nine months. More complex programs do both, setting up sequences of parallel projects responsible for creating a progression of complex deliverables. Establishing programs is discussed in Problems 21, 26, and 46.

If the initial planning process generates hundreds of separate activities, the basic work breakdown process may be used along with affinity analysis or some other approach for grouping similar work to create a logical set of largely independent subprojects. If the project is larger than this, or larger than you prefer, the first step might be to work from subcomponents of the overall deliverable to initiate separate work breakdown structures, for components in parallel or interim deliverables in parallel (or both), where the scoping for each is sized to enable thorough planning and ongoing control. Whatever the approach, the ultimate goals are to set up manageable projects that include all the work needed.

Finding Project Leaders

Decomposition into projects that can be handled well is part of the battle. Each project also must be delegated to a project leader who will take responsibility for the work, and assigned to a team capable of doing the work. Some programs assume that the management part is easy and can be done by the program manager, so the team leaders can be mostly technical and need not be bothered much with "project management stuff." For small programs that have only a few teams this might work, but even here it is risky to delegate the projects to individuals lacking the skills and aptitudes that good project management requires. Calling subject matter experts project managers does not necessarily make them good project leaders; there is more to it than that, especially in the context of a large, complex program. Select the leaders of the projects making up the program carefully, seeking adequate experience and competence. The composition of each project team also matters, so work with the project leaders to determine the needed skills and staffing for each project.

Treat the initial program breakdown as a draft, and work with the project leaders and their contributors through several iterations of planning to ensure that the work is well defined, balanced across the projects, and adequately staffed.

Managing Project Connections

Large, complex projects solve one problem through decomposition and delegation, but they create another one. The resulting projects are generally treated as independent, and if you structure the program well they largely will be. They are never actually independent, however, and all the interdependencies must be identified and managed. These connections or interfaces are primarily the responsibility of the program manager, and managing them is discussed in Problems 55 and 56.

These interfaces and all other pertinent program data should be gathered and stored centrally, where all who need them can find and use them. A discussion of this is included in Problem 46. Ensure that all contributors can drill down to information related to their work with little difficulty. The more that people can operate independently, the less likely it will be that program progress will be held up while waiting for you or someone else to dig out the answer to a question.

A central principle of successful program management is focusing primarily on the details that involve the program as a whole. No single person can keep up with thousands of activities and the efforts of hundreds of contributors, but you can track dozens of project interfaces; the general progress of a core team of capable project leaders; and the major risks, issues, and other matters that affect the overall program. Surviving a large program relies on aggregating and delegating most of the detail to others, where it can and will be managed competently.

48. How can I get meaningful commitment from team members that ensures follow-through?

Project management depends on successful delegation, as discussed in several earlier problems. This rests on clear assignment of ownership, offering of something in return, and diligent tracking.

Assigning Ownership

Motivation in the workplace has been studied for decades, and one finding that has been repeatedly verified, not surprisingly, is that people are most enthusiastic about work that they enjoy and that they are responsible for. Project leaders often complain that their team members mostly (or all) work for others, so they are not able to really control anything. Although you may not be able to manipulate salaries, assign workspaces, or directly do other management functions, these factors are not as important to motivation as many assume. The work itself, responsibility, achievement, and recognition are all generally more important, and as project leaders we can control or strongly influence all of them. Securing a commitment relies on knowing enough about your contributors to make assignments that exploit their preferences for work and achievement, which is one of the key reasons for establishing good relationships.

As you proceed with planning and creating a work breakdown structure for your project, observe which of your team members are most interested in each part of the project. When it comes time to assign owners, ask for volunteers and as much as possible align the assignments with the interests of your project staff.

Some work on the project will be very desirable and other work probably far less so. Never assume that work you find uninteresting will be equally unappealing to others, though. There may be someone on your team who loves writing documentation or other work that others would flee the room to avoid, so always ask and let people sort themselves into assignments that they desire insofar as you are able.

Involving the team in planning is a good way to get a sense of where

118

people's interests lie, and as the work profile develops you can get a good feel for which areas of the project are best understood by which members of your team. Getting a reliable commitment for activities that people want to do is often little more than asking and attaching a name.

Staffing "Orphan" Activities

All the work needs an owner, even the activities that no one seems to want to do. As you are allocating owners to project activities, investigate why no one seems interested in taking responsibility for some of them. If the primary reason is that no one knows how to do it, you may find someone who would gladly take it on if offered a chance to learn how. If it is undesirable because it seems overwhelming, you might find willing owners for pieces of it following further breakdown. If an activity seems unpopular because no one believes it is necessary, investigate, and if this is correct, drop it. If no one has enough time to take on the work, perhaps additional staffing or adjustment of priorities is in order. There are many other reasons for people to be reluctant to sign up for project work, so you need to probe to find out why. If there is some way to deal with it and locate a willing owner, do so.

Other necessary project work inevitably falls to the bottom of the list because it is dull, is thankless, depends on working with difficult people, or for whatever reason seems unappealing. Because it is needed, someone will have to do it. Securing a reliable commitment in these cases will require some negotiating skills and some "giving and getting." One thing you can consider, as mentioned above, is the opportunity to learn something new. You also might be able to bundle the work as a "package deal" with other project assignments that are attractive. If you get creative, there is a wide spectrum of other things you can potentially offer, such as personal favors, covering some of the project management overhead for the person willing to accept responsibility, or anything else you can mutually agree to.

If you are unable to secure an owner, even after your best efforts to cajole, investigate whether there might be a different, more desirable way to get a similar result. In some cases, outsourcing the work on a contract basis might also be an option. Consult other project leaders who have taken on similar projects to find out how they have handled similar situations. Discussing problematic work within your project with your sponsor or stakeholders might generate some viable options, too.

As an absolute last resort, you can even consider taking responsibility for some of these activities yourself, depending on your availability and background to do it. This may eat into time more needed for project management work, though, and you will run the risk that on future projects no one will need to volunteer for "scut work"; you will do all of it. You will find some guidance on when this might be appropriate in Problem 49.

Tracking the Work

Reliable commitments depend on diligent tracking, so plan to collect and report on status at least weekly. You will have to keep an eye especially on any work that is not very desirable or that you may have assigned to anyone suspected to be undependable. You can find some helpful ideas for dealing with due-date slippages in Problem 43.

49. As a project manager, what should I delegate and what should I do myself?

Depends on:
- ▲ Project and team size
- ▲ Skills and experience available on your team

As discussed earlier, project management responsibilities are generally yours for any project where you are the designated leader. Delegation of some of this work to others can be necessary and appropriate on very large programs, but for the most part it is best to "delegate" all of it, or at least the most essential parts, to yourself.

Project leaders can safely assume that their project management responsibilities will consume roughly 10 percent of their time per contributor on their teams. This time is consumed in meetings, communications, care and feeding of stakeholders, problem solving, hand-holding, and other general project-related tasks. If your team is larger than about nine people (whether they all report directly to you or not), you won't have much bandwidth available to take on other assigned work. Even part-time contributors count—even though they might theoretically require less attention, often they actually require more because of their distractions and other priorities.

Assessing Your Potential Availability

Your project will probably be your primary responsibility, but it may not be your only one. Consider how much time any other work you are committed to will require, and include that with the overall assessment of your workload. Also include any planned time off or other interruptions such as organizational meetings that will take time away from your project. If you have only modest other demands on your time and your project is small, or you have a very experienced and competent team that will require little attention, you may find that you do have some amount of time to devote to other assigned work on the project.

In gauging your capacity, it's prudent not to schedule more than about 90 percent of your time in advance; you will need to be able to react quickly to problems and issues as they arise.

Delegating Project Work to Yourself

Even if you do appear to have some available work capacity, set a target to delegate nearly all the project activities you define to your contributors. Consider yourself a last resort, and only assign yourself work that is easily interrupted and not schedule critical. Your first priority should be to the project as a whole, and if you assign yourself critical work you are liable to find yourself with conflicting top priorities.

You may find that there are activities for which you are by far the most qualified and experienced person on your team. Even for this work, you should not consider yourself as the first option. It is difficult to assign work to people who are less competent than you are, and it can be painful to watch people fumbling through tasks that you can do blindfolded. If you intend to take the role of project leadership seriously, you need to get over this. Assigning work to your team members will build the base of skills on your team, and it will leave you open to help and mentor as needed in addition to all your other responsibilities.

In short, assign to yourself scheduled activities (other than those directly related to project management) only when you have available capacity, the work is noncritical, and you appear to be the only reasonable option.

Remaining Flexible

Throughout your project, things will happen that won't be as you planned them. The main reason for leaving some available capacity for yourself unscheduled is so you will be able to take on unanticipated, emergency work as the need arises. If a key contributor is out ill or otherwise indisposed, someone will need to step in. Effective project leaders are always assessing the overall status and rebalancing the work in the face of reality, so that progress can continue more or less as planned. Delegating work to yourself during the project is nearly inevitable, and if your "normal" workload consumes all of your capacity, the only option open to you will be to work overtime. If you plan to see much of your home and family during your projects, exercise great restraint when delegating planned work to yourself.

50. Who should estimate activity durations and costs?

Depends on:
- ▲ Staff experience
- ▲ Project novelty
- ▲ Consequences of estimating errors

Project estimation is a complicated process, and for many types of projects it is not done with much accuracy. Doing it well involves the contributors who will be responsible for the work and the project leader, and may also benefit from inputs of experts, sponsors, and stakeholders. Regardless of exactly who gets involved, precision and consistency rely on good process and metrics, which are explored in Problems 51 and 52.

Establishing Objectives

Before any detailed, activity-level estimating can be done, there will be high-level estimates for the project as a whole established by the project sponsor and stakeholders involved in initiation. If the assumed cost and duration are not consistent with the expected benefits and value, no project will ever exist. These estimates may be based on some analysis, or they may be wild guesses pulled out of the air; whatever their basis, these initial estimates should be treated only as general goals. Although they may also represent some known constraints, the initial top-down estimates can be used only as provisional starting points. Setting a realistic project baseline requires thorough planning, analysis, and detailed estimates developed by the team responsible for the work.

Involving Activity Owners

Project planning relies on good requirements definition and scoping, involving the stakeholders as explored in Problem 22. The resulting scope for the project provides the basis for a work breakdown structure, which at its lowest level defines the tasks that must be done to complete the project. Each of these tasks will need both a duration and a cost (or effort) estimate, and the best source for the initial bottom-up estimates will be the assigned activity owner plus any other contributors involved.

The first consideration for estimating will be the method chosen to do the work. Effort and duration estimates depend strongly on the approach and process to be used for the work, so once this is clear, bottom-up estimates are possible. Other considerations for the initial estimates include potential risks and any remaining unknowns, such as any contributors who will be involved but are not yet assigned.

Involving Others

For work where there is ample precedent and a lot of experience, the estimates provided by those who will do the work may be more than adequate. For work that is novel or where you lack experience, you may want to get outside assistance. Involving peers in your own organization or networking with contacts in professional societies may provide useful information. Even getting quotations or proposals from outside service providers (whether you are considering outsourcing the work or not) can provide potentially useful insight. Again, additional considerations will include risks and unknowns, such as just how comparable the experiences and metrics developed elsewhere will be to your particular situation.

Adding Your (Skeptical) Inputs

The final arbiter of project estimates needs to be you, as the project leader, because ultimately it's your project. In examining the initial estimates, be skeptical of any that appear either too conservative or too optimistic. Ask questions about the basis for the cost and duration estimates, and probe to uncover exactly how the work is to be done. If you are not convinced that the people providing the estimates know enough about the work, ask more questions. Especially if the estimates seem too small, challenge the owner to break the work down further (whether you intend to track at that level or not).

Compare the duration and cost estimates, and test if they are consistent given what you know about how the work will be staffed. If they are not consistent, provide guidance for adjusting the cost estimate, the duration estimate, or both. If staffing commitments for all of the work are not in place, collect range estimates that will be refined later when the skill sets of the contributors are known. If there are known risks associated with the work, include an appropriate margin for reserve (to be managed by you for the project as a whole, not to "pad" activity estimates).

Finally, compare the bottom-up detailed estimates of cost to the top-down objectives for project expense to see how much trouble you are in. Consider options that might make sense for bringing costs more into line with expectations if the variance is significant. Use the duration estimates to build a preliminary schedule and test it against your project's timing goals. Again, if there are substantial differences, revisit options that might realistically reduce durations (and also revisit workflow and dependency assumptions, as discussed in Problem 54). In all cases where your estimates exceed your initial constraints, document the information that you will need to negotiate a realistic baseline with your sponsor before formally committing to a fixed project objective.

51. How do I improve the quality and accuracy of my project estimates?

Better estimates, whether of durations or costs, rely on involving the right people, using metrics, and having a good process. This problem focuses on the process; staffing and metrics are addressed in Problems 50 and 52, respectively. Good process contributes to the quality of estimates, but accuracy ultimately depends on the estimates being both *believable* (which is where measurement comes in) and *believed* (particularly by those who must deliver on them).

Selecting Methods

The starting point for all project estimating begins with determining the work methods. Before you have thought through the task at hand and determined a credible plan of attack for completing it, any estimating you do will just be a wild guess. To determine with any precision how long an activity will take and what it will cost, you must be able to describe what will be done and who will do it. If you have activities for which you have no idea how to proceed, you will need to either figure it out as part of your project planning or note it as a potential show stopper risk. As you are considering approaches for each task, challenge any assumptions about how it "must be done" and search for efficiencies, valid shortcuts, or other opportunities that could realistically save time, effort, or even both.

Once you have a reasonable idea of how your team will approach the work, there are a number of possible estimating techniques. Which methods apply best depends on at least two factors: your experience with the work, and the quality and relevance of any available historical data. The table on the next page summarizes some common estimating processes.

The best case is for work you have completed before where you were paying attention. If your team has both relevant experience and relevant metrics, estimating duration and cost should be straightforward and may require little more than simply looking up some figures from past projects. If an activity is similar to past work but differs in scale, you may have to estimate by adjusting your past measurements

	Relevant metrics exist	*No data is available*
Prior activity experience	• Project retrospectives • Databases • Notes and status reports • Parametric formulas and experiential rules ("size methods")	• Task owner and team inputs • Peer inputs • Inspections • Delphi analysis • Short ("2- to 20-workday" or "80-hour") WBS activities • Further breakdown
No activity experience	• Published information • Vendor quotes • Expert consultation	• Guesses • Doing part and extrapolating • Outside help • Older methods

to account for any "size" differences. For software projects, size may be gauged in noncommented lines of code, function points, or similar units. For other projects, counting pieces, components, block diagram elements, or other activity deliverable factors may be used to correct estimates based on earlier experiences. Always be a little skeptical when adjusting estimates based on size adjustments; the estimates of "size" for the current project may be little more than wild guesses themselves. The precision of an estimate can never be any better than its least accurate input.

The next best case is the upper-right quadrant, where the work is familiar, but for some reason no one has ever kept any records. (In the long run there is really not much excuse for this, but in the short run it happens. Good project leaders strive to avoid this.) For activities of this type, you may be able to get useful estimates by consulting others in your organization (who may be more methodical in their note taking). You can also base your estimates on anecdotal and other information available within your team. Involvement and thorough understanding of relatively small pieces of work is fundamental to good estimating anyway, and for many project tasks the estimates that emerge from discussing and planning the work can be quite accurate. Collaborative estimating techniques such as Delphi—where individual estimates are collected from a group of people, clustered, and then discussed—are also effective ways of tapping into historical information that is stored in people's memories instead of a database. These estimating ideas are also good means for validating estimates that are initially derived from documented empirical data.

Because projects are all different and there will inevitably be at least some work that is new, you will have at least a few activities where your team will have little or no relevant experience. Don't assume that just because you have no experience with a type of work, no one does; there may be useful information external to your team that you can tap into. Research on the Web or consultations with outside experts may provide an adequate basis for fairly good estimates. When using estimating data from elsewhere, consider any significant environmental or infrastructure differences and adjust accordingly. Someone else's past experiences may differ substantially from those on your current project. Nevertheless, even external information is generally a great deal more useful than none at all.

The worst case is work where you have no experience and apparently no one has any data. Here, the most popular project estimating technique—guessing—is the primary method. With reasonable care in planning and analysis, the number of such activities on a given project will only be a small portion of the overall project, and even for these there are techniques that can sometimes provide reliable estimates. For some activities, you may be able to develop useful metrics by doing a portion of the work. Working from what you learn, you can use your data to estimate the duration and cost of the work that remains. Other novel work planned for your project may be optional; there may be tried-and-true older methods that could achieve the needed results. Substituting activities you understand better will yield better estimates, lower project risk, and higher team confidence. Outsourcing the work could be another possibility in some situations where the work is unfamiliar, but you may still be dealing with unreliable estimates unless you have very good reason to believe the commitments that are made by those contracted to do the work.

Verifying Estimates

Before integrating any estimates into your plans, compare the effort and duration assessments for each activity. Consider what you know about staffing, time commitments, other work, and any time off scheduled for your team to determine if the estimates are consistent. When analyzing duration, use a realistic number of hours devoted to project activities per workday. It's best to use a percentage for available time based on your past experiences, but if you lack relevant data use the general rule of "about two-thirds."

If your time and effort estimates are not consistent (such as a two-day duration for an activity expected to require eighty hours of effort that will be done by a single person) adjust one estimate or the other (or both) to align them. Also check that your cost estimates for each activity include both any additional expenses associated with the work and the cost of the estimated effort for the contributors involved.

Also consider risks by investigating worst cases. After you have collected duration estimates for all the work identified, discuss each activity with its owner and ask what might go wrong or cause the work to take longer. If what you hear seems very probable, consider increasing the estimates. If you learn about possible failure modes that are relatively unlikely but still significant, note them as risks. If the consequences of a potential problem are particularly severe, think about other work methods or approaches that could avoid the risk. If there is a better option, adopt it and reestimate the work based on your modified plans.

For the project as a whole, check that the effort (and cost) estimates in total are generally in line with the actual results of previously completed similar projects. If the totals seem too small, revisit any estimates that appear to be excessively optimistic. Missing project activities in the initial plans is a frequent reason that projects are underestimated. Also carefully examine the work breakdown structure of any projects where the overall estimates seem too small, to check for required project work that is not yet included.

52. What metrics will help me estimate project activity durations and costs?

Project estimates are predictive metrics, and because they are forecasts about the future they tend to be somewhat imprecise. You can improve them substantially over time, however, by collecting actual measurements at the end of completed projects. These retrospective metrics provide feedback to improve your estimating processes, outlined in Problem 51, and to increase the confidence of those involved in estimating, discussed in Problem 50.

Assessing Actual Activity Performance

At the activity level, the status you collect throughout the project will either confirm the predictions in your plans or clearly show where you were in error. There are many metrics useful for this, including basic status measures such as:

▲ Actual activity durations
▲ Actual activity effort consumption
▲ Actual activity costs
▲ Performance to standard estimates for standard project activities
▲ Variances in travel, communications, equipment, outsourcing, or other estimated expenses
▲ Number of added, unplanned activities

Estimation in aggregate is also useful. Metrics for evaluating your planning process as a whole include:

▲ Total project duration
▲ Total project effort
▲ Total project cost
▲ Cumulative overtime
▲ Staff turnover and added staff
▲ Life-cycle phase effort percentages
▲ Earned value management (EVM) and related measures

The first several are simply aggregations of activity-level metrics. Project duration, effort, cost, and overtime measures are useful in detecting problems with the thoroughness and accuracy of your overall planning process. Variance in these metrics can reveal gaps or inadequacies in what you know about your projects. Possibilities for reducing the inconsistencies include process improvement, allocating more effort to project planning, and doing a better job of risk management. Unexpected staff turnover or adding staff can also lead to significant estimating problems, because dealing with midproject learning curve issues usually consumes substantial unplanned time and effort.

Life-cycle measures are useful for spotting underestimates and missing work in project plans. Similar projects over time tend to have comparable "shapes," with effort percentages that fall into predictable patterns that vary little from project to project. By comparing the percentages of work in each phase of plans under construction with those collected from previously completed projects, you can identify significant omissions and other problems.

When comparing your plans against norms, check whether there is a disproportionate amount of effort allocated to "development" (or whatever the phase of your life cycle is called where most of the work is done to actually create the deliverable). People associate most strongly with this part of their projects—it's where programmers program, carpenters build stuff, writers write, and in general, where all of us do whatever it is that we say our job is. Because people tend to focus on this, it is not unusual for this part of the plan to be fairly complete and well estimated. The rest of the plan gets less attention and may be severely underestimated, either out of inattention or through wishful thinking. Nevertheless, all the work is real and even the tasks that are initially missing from unpopular portions of the project will have to be completed before closing the project. Failing to identify (or underestimating) them won't change this. As the planning process comes to completion, check the relative percentages across all the life-cycle phases before baselining your project. If the "development" phase or phases represents a higher percentage of the overall work than is typical, look for the work you have missed in the other life-cycle phases.

Also look for the relative balance between early project analysis and late-project testing, in both your current project and the norms from your post-project metrics. When too little attention is devoted to early project phases, the inevitable price to be paid will be a large late-project work bulge. When you start your project with a solid understanding of what your project is, the closure phase will involve a lot less thrash. You will significantly reduce rework, have fewer remedial efforts to complete work you missed, and experience less overall trouble finishing your project.

The last item listed, EVM, can be quite controversial in project management circles. EVM involves substantial planning overhead, and frankly, there are many projects for which the cost of a full "bells-and-whistles" implementation will dwarf the value it provides to the project leader. Although this is hard to disagree with, there may be other considerations. For projects done on a contract basis, and especially for those where it is mandatory, the planning and status information required for EVM implementation will be (or certainly should be) readily available. Even for other projects, much of the foundation required for EVM is included in basic planning.

EVM basically concerns only three metrics: planned value (PV), actual cost (AC), and earned value (EV). PV is a predictive metric based on cumulative activity cost estimates, evaluated across the project timeline. This is something that emerges easily from the cost (or effort) estimates that project leaders should be developing anyway, and should be easily derived from the project baseline. At the project deadline, PV is equal to the "budget at completion" because all estimated project costs will have been accumulated by the end of the project. AC is a similar metric, but it is diagnostic, evaluated as the project runs from the collected status. AC is the sum of all costs (or, again, effort) accumulated by the project up to the current status date. Although not every project collects effort/cost data as part of weekly status, it can be very useful to do so.

The problem that EVM attempts to solve is that even if you set PV for the project's entire run and evaluate AC with each weekly status, you can't learn much by directly comparing them. If there is a difference between these metrics, the cause might be due to a timing factor, a cost factor, or some combination. In fact, even when your project is in trouble these two metrics can be the same, as long as the effects of the timing and cost factors offset each other.

EV is the third metric in EVM, and it was created to deal with this quandary. EV combines the estimated costs (same as PV) with the actual schedule performance (same as AC). As a result, we can compare EV with AC, and if there is a difference it must be due to a variance between the expected and actual cumulative costs for the completed work—the timing information is always the same. If there is a difference between EV and PV, this result can only be due to a difference in schedule performance for the same reason. The table on the next page shows how these three metrics relate to one another and to your project's two schedules and two budgets.

	Budgets	
Schedules	Planned Expenses	Actual Expenses
Planned Schedule	Planned Value (PV)	
Actual Schedule	Earned Value (EV)	Actual Cost (AC)

Evaluating EV at any point in the project requires only the status data needed for PV and AC. If you are already collecting this data, implementing EVM need not be difficult.

Even if you are not collecting status data at this level of detail, you can still devise a "poor man's" rough equivalent that can be used for nearly any project. EVM allocates the total project budget bit by bit to your project activities, based on estimated size. You could also devise a much simpler approximation, however, where the budget (or total effort) is spread evenly—if there are 100 activities, each gets 1 percent of the budget. Early in the project the distortion this causes may be substantial, because the difference between the accumulated simple average costs and cumulative activity cost estimates is likely to be significant for such a tiny number of tasks. As the project progresses, though, the number of activities grows and the accumulated results, both planned and actual, will converge with the average (especially if you observed the work breakdown structure guidelines and most of your project activities are of similar size).

There are dozens of additional metrics associated with EVM, but all are compound metrics involving the basic three: PV, AC, and EV. It's possible to get so complicated with EVM that it makes your head explode, but obtaining useful information for project tracking and improving your estimation processes using something like EVM need not be overwhelming.

53. How can I realistically estimate durations during holidays and other times when productivity decreases?

Depends on:
▲ Project length
▲ Geographical distribution of the team
▲ Project urgency

Identifying Holidays

If you have team members who work in different locations or for different organizations, ask about their holiday schedules. You might be able to find Web pages containing such information, but it is always better to ask. In some locales not everyone takes every holiday, and there may also be "personal holidays" that you should know about. Around major holidays productivity is likely to deteriorate, so use historical information to adjust durations estimates on activities around these periods, such as for work done at year-end in the United States, Europe, and other locations where people will probably be distracted by Christmas, New Year's, and other festivities. In Asia, be sensitive to the impact of the Lunar New Year (and note that like Easter it moves around on the calendar from year to year). Also be skeptical of any significant milestones that fall near these major holidays, the ends or beginnings of school years, or other times when people are likely to be away from work.

Accounting for Other Project Absences

As part of your estimating process, collect vacation schedules from your team. On longer projects, place reminders in your calendar to refresh your vacation schedules at least once per quarter. Request that the members of your team inform you as soon as possible when they learn about jury duty, doctor's appointments, military service, family responsibilities, or any other obligations that will take them away from work and your project.

You also need to schedule project work around organizational events and dates. Inquire about any upcoming "all hands" meetings that are scheduled, and note their dates. Consider any impact of the fiscal boundaries such as quarter- or year-ends, and any other important dates in your organization. If any particular dates are likely to affect your project, adjust your estimates to schedule around them.

As the expected timing for specific activities takes shape, note and resolve any conflicts with your contributors' scheduled time off and other date-related issues. Work with the task owner to adjust the estimates, extending the durations as needed to reflect when people will and won't be available. Relocate key project milestones that fall near important external dates to more realistic time frames.

No matter how thorough your plans are, you will never have perfect information. Things happen, including illnesses, emergencies, and even things that people are aware of but forgot to tell you about. Establish some schedule reserve at the project level to deal with this, sized using typical project experience with unanticipated absences from recent projects.

54. How can I develop realistic schedules?

Depends on:
- ▲ Project scale
- ▲ Project novelty
- ▲ Team commitment

Establishing a Foundation for Scheduling

Realistic schedules require thorough work breakdown structures containing activities of modest size at their lowest level of detail. Use guidelines such as "no larger than eighty hours of effort" or "durations between two and twenty days" to ensure that your granularity will be appropriate for realistic control and monitoring of your planned work. You may need to break up very large projects into subprojects to build useful schedules; practical schedules generally have no more than approximately 200 activities. It is very unlikely that you will be able to manage your project well if your scheduled tasks are too big or if you have too many of them.

Good schedules also rely on good estimates. Factors to consider for creating better estimates are found in Problems 50 to 53.

Sequencing the Work

Armed with a robust list of project activities for which you have believable estimates, you have what you need to analyze the workflow. Realistic schedules are based on contiguous chains of well-defined activities and milestones. Each scheduled item should be directly linked both backward to the project start and forward to the project end. Using your duration estimates and workflow dependencies, you can define a network containing unbroken sequences of work that integrate all required project activities.

Project schedules contain activities, which are derived from the lowest level of your project work breakdown structure, and milestones, which are important "moments in time" for your project. Activities require estimates for both duration and cost/effort. Milestones are events with no duration and usually require no scheduled effort. Milestones may be used to identify the starts and ends of life-cycle phases, to synchronize related activities, and to show key external dependencies. By convention, project schedules begin with a start milestone (or a milestone with some similar name) reflecting the date when the work is expected to (or actually did) commence.

Realistic scheduling is a team process, so involve your team members in the workflow analysis process, including at least the activity owners who provided your initial estimates. Effective scheduling also benefits from creativity, so it's best done using a method that fully engages the "left brain." Scheduling a project by yourself, hunched over a computer screen, will guarantee that you will miss things—probably significant things. Alternatively, using yellow sticky notes on a wall, whiteboard, or large piece of paper allows you to move things around, see the emerging big picture, simultaneously engage a team of collaborators, and remain flexible. Gather your team members where you have space to spread things out and begin your scheduling process with a sticky note for your start milestone.

Select every defined activity in your project that has no work that must precede it and link it backward to the start milestone using a pencil (or something else you can easily erase). Continue this process by linking activities to work that must precede it, adding milestones into your evolving network as necessary, until all project activities are accounted for and each is part of a continuous path connecting the start and an end milestone marking the end of the project.

As you progress, some links will need to be adjusted because your initial workflow assumptions may need adjustment as you incorporate new activities. In other cases you may find that two activities are connected, but not directly. In order to model project workflow, you may need to add new activity to your project work breakdown structure before it can be interposed between the already identified tasks. You may also find activities that need to be broken into separate parts that are separated in your network. Consider scenarios and focus on the questions, "What do we need to do before we can begin this?" and "What comes next, following the completion of this task?" Add work as necessary, striving to build a contiguous network of activities showing credible sequences of work that will enable you to complete the project. Update your project work breakdown structure to reflect any modifications made during the scheduling process.

Avoiding Fixed-Date Schedules

Once you have a network of linked activities that appears to be reasonable on a wall somewhere, you will likely want to enter it into a project management computer tool. (Software tools for scheduling are discussed in Problem 97.) Scheduling tools allow a wide variety of modeling techniques, including the linked dependencies of predecessor/successor workflow analysis discussed here. These schedules are very useful for tracking, control, and "what if" planning.

Computer tools also allow you to build project plans with "must start on" and "must end on" logic, but for the most part this is a bad idea. Fixed-logic schedules, like activity estimates that are unrealistically forced into line with constraints, are not all that useful because they don't model what you expect to occur. Such "schedule to fit" plans tend to be mostly wishful thinking. In addition, if the necessary workflow is not modeled using a linked network, you will be unable to determine the consequences of any slippages or proposed changes that occur in your project. Nailing your activities to arbitrary calendar dates may look like a plan and appear to meet the overall timing objectives, but if it's unrealistic it really helps no one.

It's best to develop a bottom-up schedule for your project based on logical workflow and credible duration estimates, and enter that into the computer. If the resulting end date fails to meet the initially stated goals, explore alternatives for linking the work that could realistically shorten your timeline. If your best analysis leads you to the conclusion that your project will take longer than desired, document your plans as they are and use the data in negotiating necessary adjustments before establishing your project baseline as discussed in Problem 78.

55. How can I thoroughly identify and manage external dependencies?

Nearly every project has at least some external dependencies. At least the initial request and the final deliverable generally involve a connection to parties outside of the project. In addition, there may be myriad other outside connections, for parts, information, decisions, and many other external dependencies. Managing these connections starts with identification, and it relies on meaningful commitments and tracking.

Identifying External Dependencies

The most important external dependencies for most projects involve the initial requirements and the ultimate acceptance of the project deliverable. Ideas for managing customer and stakeholder expectations are found in Problem 22.

For projects that are part of a larger program, there are many external connections to the other related projects in the program. Dealing with program interconnections is discussed in Problems 26 and 56.

For both of these situations and for all other external dependencies, the first step is to examine all inputs required before project activities begin to isolate those outside your control. For the inputs that are deliverables from other project activities, establish a predecessor/successor dependency linkage in your own project network, as discussed in Problem 54. For inputs within your own project, specifications may be somewhat informal, but they should be sufficient to ensure that the handoff results in smooth continuation of the project workflow. For any inputs that are external to your project, however, you'll need to be explicit and precise, including any mandatory performance criteria. Also include any timing and other information related to external inputs.

Some of your activities will also create outputs that will be used outside your project. Also document specifications and expected timing for your external deliverables.

Effective planning strives for a thorough understanding of all project activities. One way to ensure this is to create a "WBS dictionary" in a computer scheduling tool (or some other database or spreadsheet). This is an effective way to collect and maintain information related to all the tasks you need to manage. One approach for organizing all this data is the "ETVX" (Entry, Task, Validation, Exit) model. "Entry" includes all the inputs you require, internal and external, to your project. "Exit" specifies all of your expected outputs. "Task" and "Validation" provide information on the work you will need for estimation, execution, and control. Using such a structure, you can easily gather all of your external inputs and outputs for specific attention.

Negotiating Commitments

Once you have your external dependencies identified and documented, confirm them. For approvals and decisions, work with your sponsor, management, and stakeholders to set expectations and deadlines related to what you will need and when you will need it. For specifications, documentation, or other information that must flow into or out of your project, approach your partners and come to an agreement about specifics and due dates. Obtain specific agreement from the provider of each required input, whether tangible (parts, components, equipment) or intangible (documentation, software, process information). For inputs that come from outside of your organization, document each agreement with a contract, a purchase order, or other legal document. For contracts covering project deliverables, consider adding terms for incentives and penalties that might increase the probability that you will have what you need on time. For any inputs that are external to your project but inside your organization, exchange a "memo of understanding" or similar commitment document to verify your shared understanding of what is needed and when. If you have difficulty coming to agreement on any of your inputs, escalate the matter to your sponsor or other management to secure the agreements you need, or seek other options for meeting your needs. Resolve everything you can through commitments during your planning. If you don't, you'll need to do so later during execution—and by then it may be too late.

If, even after securing a formal commitment, you are not confident about the delivery of any critical external inputs, consider exploring other alternatives. In some situations, you may want to switch to another provider. For others you might consider obtaining a redundant commitment from another provider in addition to your primary supplier. Second sourcing is an important risk management tool, and it may be cheap insurance for keeping your project on track.

Document and confirm commitments for all your outputs, too. Although it may seem less important to worry about situations where others are depending on you, this is central to maintaining stakeholder support. Also, it's a small world; you may be dependent on the folks you are sending stuff to today to provide things you'll need tomorrow.

Tracking Commitments

Obtaining agreement is only half the battle. You also need to ensure performance. As the time for a required input approaches, reach out to the provider with a reminder at least a week in advance. For inputs such as decisions and approvals, include a description of the consequences of delay to your project, and if possible arrange for the authority to proceed using your own judgment if the approvals and decisions you require are not timely.

For commitments that have lengthy durations, collect meaningful status on progress periodically as the work proceeds. Find opportunities to participate in any interim testing or evaluations related to the inputs you need to verify progress.

As with all project status, diligently monitor what is going on. If problems develop with any of your external dependencies, work with your partners one-on-one to resolve them. As a last resort, escalate when necessary to deal with situations that you are unable to resolve on your own.

56. How do I synchronize my project schedules with several related partners and teams?

Large, complex projects—or programs—are typically decomposed into a set of related smaller projects to facilitate managing the work and for overall control. The structure and processes for setting up programs are discussed in Problems 21 and 26. This problem focuses on program planning and integrated scheduling. The overall process is based on each project developing a reasonable stand-alone schedule. Starting with these project schedules, you then iterate through a series of integration steps to establish a set of schedules at both the project and program levels that are logically consistent and can be used for tracking and control.

Planning Each Component Project

After establishing a first-cut decomposition of a large program into projects, the program manager must find a competent leader for each one. These leaders should be experienced with the work to be done and take full responsibility for their pieces of the overall program. Each project leader also will lead a team of contributors who will do the work largely autonomously on their portions of the program.

The first step in program planning is to encourage the leaders to work with their team to develop a credible plan for their own project. For this, each leader will need a shared understanding of the program objectives, consistent definitions for life-cycle deliverables, and all required program testing and acceptance criteria. Integrating disparate schedules is never easy, but it can be made a lot more straightforward if you establish formatting standards in advance, provide planning templates to ensure consistency, and strongly encourage (or mandate) the use of a common computer tool to be used for all project planning. Selecting software tools for large programs is discussed in Problem 98.

For each project, the assigned project leader and staff need to develop a work breakdown structure for their work and develop estimates for the resulting activities. From this they can build their initial schedules based on all identified dependencies, both within their project and external to it.

Identify all external connections for each project using a process similar to that in Problem 55, and document each project schedule in preparation for integration into the overall program plans using the format and any computer tools set up for the program.

Iterating the Program Plans

The overall goal of program planning is to keep all of the planning efforts synchronized. Following the detailed planning efforts for each of the projects in the program, you can do a trial program schedule integration. This initial integration is typically a mess, but a thorough inspection will identify the most significant interconnection and timing problems. Using this as feedback, the next iteration will be a great deal cleaner.

One type of large program undertaken by a Hewlett-Packard division used a "Straw-Silver-Gold" process for this program and project plan integration. The process started with program decomposition and staffing, providing each project team with early program information. Each team used this information to create its initial project plans quickly. All these early project plans were then pulled together into a "Straw" program plan to see how things looked. Each project plan included a number, sometimes a large number, of external dependencies on other projects, and inevitably there were many issues related to project interconnections and timing. Nonetheless, the overall integrated program had some parts that began to look coherent, with formal agreements on the interfaces ready to be formally signed off by the project leaders involved.

The initial integration also could be used to validate all, or at least large portions, of the initial program breakdown, and highlight the most significant scheduling problems to be resolved. Sometimes this trial integration revealed that there were too many project interconnections to permit the project leaders to operate with much autonomy. In these cases, the initial program breakdown would be discarded in favor of a better program decomposition with a cleaner overall structure. This step sometimes also resulted in adjustments to the leadership and composition of project teams to align with the new program hierarchy. Using this revised program breakdown, the project leaders would try again and redo their "Straw" phase.

The output of the "Straw" planning iteration would be a quantity of loose ends and timing problems, provided as feedback to the project leaders. Based on this, the project leaders and their teams would build their improved set of "Silver" plans, which were used for the next try at program plan integration. This version was also imperfect, but the number of issues discovered in this iteration was relatively small.

Feedback from this second program planning iteration could be used for the third, "Gold," project planning iteration. The "Gold" version, usually the final one, provided the project plans from which the overall program plan could be built and baselined. It also contained documentation of all the listed cross-project dependencies and interfaces, each explicitly agreed to by both the providing and receiving project leader using a formal sign-off procedure.

Maintaining Program Plan Integration

Ongoing program and related project planning also depends on periodic review and adjustment of plans and objectives. Schedule "rolling wave" planning exercises at least every six months throughout any major program to refresh the project plans and your program-level integrated plans. Use planning reviews to pick up changes, emerging issues, new risks, and any interfaces that may have been missed in earlier planning.

57. How do I effectively plan and manage a project that involves invention, investigation, or multiple significant decisions?

By definition, all projects are unique and involve at least some aspects that have not been done before. For some projects, the changes between one and the next may be minor, and project planning may be adequately done using little more than a copy machine and a red pen. For projects where you are blazing new trails, though, there may be substantial work required for which there is little precedent. Project management processes may seem inadequate for these "bleeding-edge" efforts, but even here they help by allowing you to segregate the known aspects from the unknown and focus better on what matters most.

Defining the Project

Even on a project where you may be uncertain about the method or even the feasibility, you should still be able to outline at least the questions that need to be answered, the number of options that must be explored (at least roughly), or the number of identified issues to be resolved. You also will know about standards and process steps that have been used on past projects of similar type, and can identify some "boilerplate" activities such as preparations for management reviews and other tasks typical of recent projects.

Gather your project definition information together and work with your team to create a work breakdown structure (or at least a list) containing the activities that you are aware of that are necessary to deal with the questions, options, feasibility issues, and other aspects of the project. For each listed activity, characterize it as either a "known" (something that you can assign, estimate, schedule, and track) or an "unknown" (something where you have no clue how to proceed). Classify activities that seem to fall between the categories with the "unknowns." Get a sense of the overall magnitude of work represented by each category.

145

Planning for What You Know

For the activities that fall into the known category, confirm your activity definitions, assign an owner, and apply good project management planning and tracking processes for executing and controlling the work. If the known activities appear to represent less than half of your overall project, you might consider delegating the coordination of all of them to someone on your team, so that you will be better able to focus on the larger, unknown portions with less distraction.

In any case, applying good project processes to manage the more straightforward parts of the work will remove them from the list of things you will be constantly obsessing and worrying about, and it will reduce the overall amount of project chaos. If you use the fact that some parts of a project are difficult to plan precisely as an excuse to not plan at all, it will just make a hard project even harder.

Dealing with What You Don't Know

Even for the parts of your project that you cannot plan well, project management practices can help you to rein in some of the disorder. If the number of unknowns is very large, consider splitting the project into two projects. The initial project will be relatively small, focusing on investigation, feasibility, and answering most of the open questions. Its deliverable will be either a concrete proposal for a larger, follow-on project to deliver on the initial objective if that is a prudent business decision, or a recommendation to go no further (or to initiate an alternative investigation).

You can use your WBS (or task list) to identify skill gaps on your team. Use your skills analysis to justify adding contributors with the needed skills to your team or to get approval and plan for the training and development needed by your current team members. Your WBS may also reveal that you have insufficient staff, and can help you to justify increases in resources or a more realistic project timeline.

Some of your unknowns may be due to technological choices or other decisions that could be revisited. When viable, consider using older, better understood technologies, processes, and methods to reduce the amount of "unknown" work and improve your control.

Don't assume that what you don't know is not known to anyone. Explore what your peers inside your organization know, and network outside through professional associations or other groups to gain insight into the experiences of others. Investigate hiring or contracting experts who have relevant backgrounds that could reduce your uncertainty and risk.

If you must commit to a project that has a large amount of uncertainty, mitigate it by applying good project management practices. Identify the riskiest work, and begin it as early as possible in your project. This will provide you with the most options for dealing with problems and will allow you to shut down projects you discover are impossible with minimum investment. Also plan to start any work requiring very specialized internal expertise or outside contract help early in your project. Isolate the most difficult jobs in the project and assign them to your best, most competent, and creative people. When prudent, initiate parallel (redundant) development efforts, employing alternative methods to increase your probability of ultimate success.

Use your WBS analysis to identify and list the key questions that your project must answer or issues that must be resolved. Although you may not formally sequence this work in a traditional schedule, as time passes you can still monitor how much you have completed, how things are progressing with others, and what work you have not started. If your rate of progress is not consistent with your overall objectives, you can use this information to decide whether to stop or revise the project. (For example, if in a six-month investigation you must resolve ten issues, it might be reasonable to expect that at the three-month point, five would be completed or at least showing significant progress.) You can similarly partition high-uncertainty project work into checkpoints, with defined measures of progress to demonstrate continued, appropriate movement toward project completion. With some creative thinking, you can develop a sense of workflow for most undertakings that will reduce chaos and provide you with a means for assessing your progress. Status information such as this will also be useful for keeping your stakeholders up-to-date and help you in managing their expectations.

Set up in-depth reviews for projects having substantial unknowns approximately quarterly, and use the reviews to make decisions on further funding, continuation with project modifications, or cancellation.

58. How should I manage adoption of new technologies or processes in my projects?

Depends on:
▲ The nature of the project
▲ The experience of the team

Analyzing Costs and Benefits

Even when there are compelling reasons to adopt something new, change is never easy. Big project changes increase risk and will probably be resisted by at least some of your contributors and stakeholders, so you will need to manage these changes carefully. A prudent project leader will assess three estimates before committing to a change: the cost of remaining with the status quo, the cost of transition, and the monetary benefits of making the change.

In building the business case for a change to a new process or technology, you first must estimate the consequences of staying with your current methods. You probably have some reasonably good data on existing costs, but you may need to adjust them to reflect any projections or trends that could affect them. Work to understand any significant recent or expected shifts when developing your economic analysis of the status quo.

For both the costs and benefits of a change, your numbers will probably be far less reliable. If the estimates are provided by those in favor of the change, transition costs are likely to be optimistically minimized, and benefits may be inflated. When changes are assessed by people who are opposing them, the reverse is usually the case—costs are huge and benefits seem negligible. Good decision making requires a lot of skepticism, ensuring that the estimates for both costs and value are plausible. For the benefits estimated (which tend to be optimistically too high), it's useful to ask questions such as: "What is that estimate based on?" "What might happen that could decrease the value or effectiveness?" and "Says who?" (Well, maybe not the last one. . . .) If the benefits appear to be overblown, make your own estimates to share with your stakeholders. In verifying cost estimates for a change, check that they include any project impact that you are aware of as well as all the expenses expected with such changes.

If the overall financial analysis that emerges from your analysis is positive, embrace the change and use the business case to help build support for it. If the overall numbers are shaky, share them with your sponsor and key stakeholders. If the proposed change is not a good idea, use your influence to avoid or modify what is being proposed.

Planning Conservatively

If a major change will be part of your project, plan conservatively. Reassess the skills and knowledge necessary on your team, and be realistic about the aptitudes and interest your team members have in the change. If you need additional or different staffing, begin working with your sponsor to obtain it. In estimating, consider learning curve issues carefully, increasing estimates as necessary to deal with them. If training will be needed by any of your contributors, incorporate the funds required to pay for it in your cost estimates.

Consider all unknowns and risks carefully, and develop contingency and fallback plans to recover if you encounter problems. Also analyze worst-case scenarios, and use your data to build adequate schedule and budget reserve into your plans.

Securing Buy-In

Change is hard. Except for the parties pushing for it, most will resist it at least to some degree. To move forward with a change successfully, you'll need to build support.

If you need buy-in from your management or project sponsor, set up a meeting with them and come equipped with facts and figures. The business case will be central to these discussions, but also consider any other specific benefits of the change that will matter personally to those you report to. If the change will result in a better deliverable, a shorter project, greater efficiency, or anything else that matters to your management, document it. The more you are able to connect the benefits to things your sponsor and key stakeholders care about, the easier it will be to gain their enthusiastic approval.

If you need to get support from your peers and your team, consider this "what's in it for me?" factor from their perspective. When discussing the change, focus on anything about it that will make each individual's life better or work easier, and on its importance to your shared management. If the new technology or process is a learning experience that might be desirable, stress that. If you have success stories or specific, credible measures from any prototyping or testing that support your case, discuss them. Gaining a meaningful commitment for a successful change will require overcoming the resistance of others using credible information and your best persuasive skills.

59. How should I plan to bring new people up to speed during my projects?

Except on very short projects, you may rarely end a project with the same people you started with. Turnover, project changes, reorganizations, and many other factors can affect the composition of your team. The keys to dealing with this effectively are doing what you can to anticipate and be prepared for changes, and working through them quickly and efficiently.

Anticipating Staff Changes

As your project plans come together, consider what the impact of losing each member of your team might be. If you had to replace a specific individual, what work would be at risk? What could you do to replace the person? What would a new person need to know to effectively step into the shoes of a missing team member in terms of assignments, necessary skills, and other factors? For team members with particularly specialized skills, take this exercise very seriously, and identify when in your project losing a critical contributor would be most damaging. Develop, at least for your own use, a contingency plan outlining what you would need to do to work through any loss of key personnel.

Also scan your plans for any places where you know your team will (or might) change. If a future phase of the work requires additional workers, add activities to your schedule for bringing them into the project and up to speed. Estimate any expenses associated with hiring, training, or other direct costs of adding them to your team. Adding a significant number of people will generally occur at a life cycle or other significant milestone, so you may be able to smooth the transition by incorporating elements of a project start-up workshop into your scheduled project review meetings.

Replacing staff can happen at any time and may require a lot of your effort. This is one of many reasons it's a bad idea to overbook your own schedule. Ensure that you retain sufficient slack in your formally scheduled project responsibilities to allow for this and other unanticipated bumps in the road. As your project progresses, remain vigilant for signs of potential turnover. Minimizing turnover is essential to success-

151

ful project management and is explored more deeply in Problem 64. Remember, it's a lot easier to retain a team member than to deal with the effects of losing that person.

As you prepare to baseline your plans, incorporate adequate budget reserve for dealing with the likely costs of staff turnover in your overall provisions for dealing with project risk.

Adding New Team Members

If you do lose a contributor or for some other reason need to bring a new person into your project, integrate the new person into your team as quickly as you can. Make the time to meet and get to know the other person, shifting your other duties around if necessary. Work to build a good personal relationship and establish trust with your new contributor. Also work to connect the new person with others on your team in meetings and other interactions to build and maintain good teamwork.

If you have lost a key contributor, determine which responsibilities can be picked up by the new person, and how quickly. If there are things that the new person cannot do right away, determine who could assume responsibility and shift your plans to make best use of the talent you have available. Even if the added person is primarily taking on new activities, review your overall plans as you develop a better sense of what that person is good at and likes to do. Consider changes to your team assignments where they make sense.

It's best to add people at the start of a project and keep them together throughout the work. Unfortunately, this is not always possible. When changes bring new people into your team, make the time to rebuild cohesive teamwork and to rebalance the task assignments among your contributors. This is never easy, but failing to do it promptly can make it a lot harder and may lead to project failure.

60. How can I resolve staff and resource overcommitments?

It's common for projects to have more work than the assigned staff can complete in the time available. Dealing with this problem begins with thorough resource planning and will require adjustments to the timeline, the scope, or both.

Resource Planning

The first step in managing resource shortfall issues is identifying them. Start by documenting your project's available resource capacity. When assessing your staff availability, account for all other team member commitments outside your project, especially those of any part-time contributors. Also consult the actual resource profiles from past projects, and use these metrics to adjust your available capacity to account for illnesses, emergencies, and other inevitable absences.

As your overall project schedule and staffing plans come together, scan your overall resource requirements to identify any periods where you have insufficient staffing, equipment, or any other needed resources. For large projects, you may want to enter your timing, staffing, and other activity data accurately into a computer-based project management scheduling tool and generate automated resource histograms. For mid-range projects you could inspect your scheduled work, week by week, and enter resource information into a spreadsheet or a table. You can also do this even more simply, at least for small projects, by scanning your time-based workflow plans and imagining the project work as it progresses. Scheduling "traffic jams," where several simultaneous activities all require the same resources, are often fairly obvious.

Revising Plans

Note any significant overcommitment problems in your initial plans, and begin considering possible adjustments to remove, or at least to minimize, them. If you are fortunate, there may also be spots in your plans where some of your staff may be undercommitted. If so, shift the timing of some work to exploit the variances and better balance your staffing with your schedule. (In theory, this can also be automated using the "resource-leveling" feature of a computer-based scheduling tool. In practice, this function is the project management equivalent of a food processor: Your project will usually be chopped, sliced, and diced beyond recognition. Before you try this at home, make sure you have a backup version of your plans.) Completely resolving resource overcommitment problems this way is unusual, but it may mitigate some of them.

It may also be possible to remove some problems by reconsidering how the work is to be done. There may be options for automating or otherwise shifting the type and amount of work needed for some constrained activities. If so, evaluate any trade-offs and shift your plans as appropriate. You also may be able to come up with different methods or improved processes for some work that could relieve some of your problems. Test that the resources needed for each activity where you have an issue are indeed necessary.

For each resource stack-up problem you detect, consider all the activities that contribute to it. Evaluate each for both importance and urgency, and use this data to rank order the work from most to least critical. Ask your contributors about the relative priority of other work outside the project they are responsible for to explore potential adjustments in their schedules. If some of the work causing your resource problems is not urgent, reschedule it. If it's unnecessary, drop it.

For all of your remaining resource conflicts, document the magnitude of your problem, clearly showing the difference between what you need and what you have. Explore possible options for resolution with other managers who are involved, escalating the discussion to include stakeholders and decision makers where necessary. Work to ensure that the assignments that people carry are the most appropriate for the overall organization.

If issues remain, approach your sponsor with your data to discuss possible options for alternative staffing. Discuss the possibilities of adding additional full- or part-time staff, outsourced contract help, or other staffing changes. If this is not feasible, have alternatives available to explore, including a variant schedule showing a credible timeline based on your committed resources, and a description of the project scope that could be achieved in the time available using available staff. (You will find more on this topic in Problem 78.) Use your planning data to negotiate with your sponsor, and work together to adjust the project objective as necessary to set a credible, realistic project baseline.

61. How can I minimize the impact of scarce, specialized expertise I need for my project?

This problem is a special case of the resource overcommitment problem explored in Problem 60. Dealing with it includes the tactics discussed there, with some additional emphasis on risk management.

Identifying Unique Resource Issues

When analyzing the knowledge, skills, and aptitudes you need to complete your work successfully, take particular notice of any that are unusual or rare in your organization. If any of the critical skills needed for your project are completely unavailable, escalate the matter to your sponsor or management to get guidance on how to proceed.

If you need skills that are available but scarce, analyze their potential for impact on your project. Unusual skills tend to be costly to retain, so most organizations manage them "lean." This results in having barely enough capacity for "normal" operations, which leads to frequent queuing and delays in access. Subject matter experts for architecture, testing, specialized design, or any other area needed for a particular part of your project will frequently be located in centrally managed functional groups and shared by many projects. In many organizations it is very common to get to the start date for an activity involving one of these specialists, and then have to wait in line until the projects ahead of you are completed.

In addition to the potential for delay, you must consider that having appropriately skilled staff today is no guarantee that they will still be available when you need them. Losing special expertise does happen, through resignation, illness, and other means, and replacing them may take considerable time (and effort).

As part of your risk identification, list all project activities where you are dependent on expertise outside your core team over which you have little control or influence.

Considering Alternatives

Not every situation where your initial plans depend on skills outside of your team need remain outside of your control. As you plan your work, look for options.

You could make developing some of the skills you need within your team part of your project. Developing new skills will make your team more robust and self-reliant, and it can be very motivating for contributors who have an interest in learning them and gaining experience. If this requires training, account for the expense in your project cost estimates and the time in your duration estimates. Mentoring by the existing experts and self-study are also options, but even if no formal training will be necessary you'll still need to adjust your timing estimates to account for learning curve issues.

Outside expertise could be an option when the specialists in your own organization are fully booked. If so, start the search and contracting processes and build the required time and contract costs into your plans.

In other cases, you may be able to buy a project component suitable for your project deliverable instead of making it and relying on specialized expertise. If this is viable, replan the work and adjust your estimates accordingly.

There may be other options available. Consider any reasonable tactics that could reduce your reliance on unavailable or potentially unreliable staffing.

Managing Resource Scarcity

Anticipate the start of all activities involving specialists, and send them a reminder a week or two in advance. Ask them to advise you if they foresee any problems starting on schedule. The more lead time you have for dealing with issues, the more options you will have for resolving them.

If your project has high priority, use it to minimize your queuing problems. If you are waiting for a resource behind a less urgent project, use your priority to better align the queue with the organization's needs. If your project has a lower priority, manage stakeholder expectations accordingly and keep your exposures and risk visible. Do not use "best-case" estimates for work having significant resource dependencies where you lack control and influence. When estimating durations, account for potential subject matter expert timing delays caused by access problems. Integrate "unique resource" risks into your risk assessment and response planning, and set a realistic project baseline including adequate timing and budget reserves.

62. What is the best approach for balancing resources across several projects?

This is an issue that can occur both with large programs and with small projects. In large programs, balancing resources is necessary when staffing is shared among the linked projects that make up the program. However, the most significant issues for projects in a program tend to relate to their linked scoping, so overlapping resources are generally not the biggest issue for programs.

Resource stack-up conflicts are much more common for small projects, usually groups of small projects led by project leaders who staff them by drawing on a pool of common contributors. The only significant connection between these projects will be their shared resources; they are otherwise completely independent. Resolving resource conflicts relies on planning each project, analyzing the overall resource profile, and adjusting the plans and expectations as required.

Planning Each Project

When project leaders are faced with four (or ten, or dozens of) projects, they might make the erroneous assumption that planning is a luxury they can't afford. If all of the projects are sufficiently trivial and there are not too many, they might even get away with this—for a little while. Eventually, though, it will catch up with them. Inadequate planning will eventually cause things to crash and burn.

The level of formality need not be extreme; fast-track planning (explored in Problem 8) may prove sufficient. Your goals for planning are to determine and list the work needed and to develop a credible roadmap that reflects both your timing objectives and your resource constraints.

Armed with a sense of the staffing requirements for each project, you are prepared to tackle the aggregated resource stack-up for all of them together. Start by checking your own workload. Test whether your communication, coordination, and leadership duties for all your projects are realistic. In general, you should plan to spend about 10 percent of your time dealing with each full-time contributor you are working with, but when managing several projects you may need to allocate more. Although you can probably manage a couple small projects, perhaps even four, taking on more than six will probably drive you crazy no matter how trivial they appear to be. If there seems to be enough of you to go around, begin to analyze the available capacity of your community of contributors. Document all significant instances of overcommitment that you find.

Making Adjustments

Explore options for resolving resource shortfall issues using a process similar to that discussed in Problem 60 for dealing with insufficient resources in a single project. Begin your process by seeking any openings for rescheduling work to take advantage of opportunities where you detect any extra staffing capacity. Shift the timing of your work to exploit any overcapacity wherever possible. Also seek to better balance the workload overall with additional activity timing shifts in the various projects.

Continue your analysis by reviewing the relative priority of each project. In general, you will want to allocate and protect the resources assigned to the most important projects, slowing (or deferring altogether) those with lower perceived value or urgency. If all the projects are important, document your resource issues and approach your sponsor and stakeholders to discuss getting additional staff, funding, or whatever resources you require to deal with your constraint.

If you are unable to gain access to sufficient resources, begin to adjust your stakeholders' expectations to align with what can realistically be accomplished using the resources you do have. Before you formally commit to schedules for each of your projects, ensure that all the baselines are realistic and consistent with your committed staffing and resource capacity.

63. How can I minimize potential late-project testing failures and deliverable evaluation issues?

The best time to deal with scope verification and stakeholder approval issues is when you are setting the project scope in the first place. Managing customer expectations is discussed in Problem 22, where the importance of clarifying performance requirements and approval criteria is emphasized. Other important ideas for avoiding late-project problems include thorough planning, frequent interim evaluations, and scrupulous management of changes.

Planning Thoroughly for Testing

As your plans and final requirement definitions come together, include well-defined activities for gaining final approval. Identify the contributors who will own the testing and evaluation tasks at project close, and work with them to define, estimate, and schedule them. Allow adequate time for testing, evaluation, and defect correction in your estimates—assuming that all tests will go smoothly only works when you are very, very lucky. Review the performance and acceptance criteria with your stakeholders, and make adjustments to your plans as appropriate following any updates you agree to.

Identify scoping risks in your planning. If portions of your scoping are unclear or seem likely to change, work to stabilize them. If there are significant scoping issues that you are unable to resolve, consider a "cyclic" or "agile" approach for your project life cycle to allow you to incrementally deliver functionality and make adjustments and course corrections as you proceed.

Whether you adopt a step-by-step approach to your work or not, plan for periodic check-ins with your users, customers, and stakeholders during your project. Include scheduled reviews of proofs-of-concept, prototypes, pilots, or other interim deliverables. Encourage participation by people who will be responsible for final approval in inspections, component tests, and other early evaluations. The feedback from these activities can provide you with an early warning system for potential later (and more serious) problems.

Also, review the late-project experiences of other similar work as part of your planning. If the retrospective analyses of recently completed projects show systemic closure issues, investigate the problems to uncover the root causes. Pursue any promising opportunities you discover that could improve your testing processes.

Managing Changes

Project changes are a major source of late-project heartache. Insufficient analysis of proposed changes—or even worse, no analysis at all—can create big testing problems. Even seemingly benign, "minor" changes may result in severe unintended consequences late in the project.

To minimize this, adopt a sufficiently formal process for managing scope changes, and establish a default of "reject" for all changes proposed lacking a compelling business justification. For every change being seriously considered, evaluate potential consequences for testing. Involve the appropriate stakeholders in decisions to accept or reject any change where there could be a significant impact on testing or acceptance criteria. For changes that are adopted, revalidate any modified testing and evaluation criteria with your users, customers, and stakeholders, and update all relevant project documentation.

64. How do I anticipate and minimize project staff turnover?

Project staffing is rarely static. The more stable it is, though, the easier it will be to finish your project. Holding on to staff involves both monitoring for and proactively managing potential turnover.

Monitoring for Signs of Restlessness

Some types of projects rarely lose people, and other types lose them all the time. Consider what is normal for your organization and plan accordingly. If your projects are short, your organization is stable, and people appear happy, you shouldn't need to worry a great deal about turnover. If your project is lengthy or there has recently been a lot of organizational churn, however, it's a good idea to keep your eyes open for potential problems.

As your project progresses, monitor your team's behavior. Individuals often behave poorly before announcing that they are leaving, so bad attitudes are often a good early warning sign of imminent turnover. If one of your contributors is resistant to your efforts to establish relationships and build trust, be wary. Lack of enthusiasm in planning and other collaborative work is also a bad sign. Chronic lateness to meetings and missing commitments are other symptoms of disengagement. In extreme cases of bad behavior, conflicts erupt, leading to poor cooperation, arguments, and fights. Ironically, the opposite of this, ready agreement to anything, is also potentially problematic. This can signal a loss of interest in what is going on; ideally your project team members should always be willing to provide serious feedback in discussions, including at least some constructive criticism.

People preparing to leave are often actively job hunting. Visible signs of this include frequent, poorly explained absences; leaving copies of their resume accidentally on copiers or shared printers; and dressing more nicely than usual. Although none of this may prove with any certainty that one of your team members is planning to quit soon, bad attitudes and apparent job hunting are always worth investigating.

Managing Proactively

If you detect signs of potential turnover, set up a meeting with the individuals involved. You may not want to confront the issue of their possible resignation directly, but telltale behaviors you have noticed can provide you with a useful place to start. If there are problems such as lateness, lack of follow-through on project commitments, or inappropriate absenteeism, ask about them. Inquire if there are particular things that are annoying your team member that could be causing these behaviors.

If you are concerned but there is nothing overt happening, a little "management by wandering around" (discussed in Problem 44) is a great way to explore if your team members are unhappy, and if they are, to dig into whatever is bothering them. Ask about anything that your contributors would like to see changed, and request suggestions for how these things might be improved. What you discover may be under your control. If so, consider changing it. Even if it is not something you can do anything about directly, you may be able to influence others, or at least provide feedback about the situation within your organization. Sometimes simply discussing situations that are bothering people will go a long way toward lowering the temperature.

If you discover that you have a team member who is about to resign and his or her continued involvement is particularly important, there may be actions you can take to protect your project. If you request it, some contributors may agree to postpone their resignation in order to avoid leaving you and the rest of your team in the lurch. In some circumstances, there may be something you could offer in exchange for their continued participation through the end of the project, or at least through its current phase. With the approval from your sponsor or management, you may even be able to arrange for special compensation or other tangible reward for staying longer.

If you reach the conclusion that losing someone is inevitable, be proactive in preparing to replace the person. Tips for adding staff to your project are discussed in Problem 59.

65. How can I avoid having too many meetings?

One of the top complaints about projects is "too many meetings." Dealing with this effectively involves structuring meetings well and eliminating unnecessary meetings.

Building Better Meetings

People hate meetings less when they are more useful and shorter. Every meeting should have a point and be only as long as necessary to achieve its stated goals.

As project leader, you will need two kinds of regular meetings: team meetings including everyone and one-on-one meetings with each contributor. For most projects, both types will be scheduled weekly. The primary objectives for these meetings are general communications and team building, and for these neither needs to be lengthy.

A one-hour team meeting should be the maximum. Test the theory that your team needs to meet every week by skipping a week. If that works, reschedule the meeting to be biweekly. (It's a bad idea to meet much less than this, though. People may start to forget who is on the team.)

Half-hour, weekly one-on-one meetings with your team members are generally sufficient, especially if you supplement them with other frequent discussions and conversations. Weekly contact with the people on your team is really about the minimum for keeping them engaged and helping them remember that they are on your project. If your team is global, schedule each one-on-one phone meeting during your contributor's workday, not necessarily during yours.

Other project meetings will be necessary but should be rare. Special-purpose meetings such as project start-up workshops can be longer, but most other specific meetings can be kept to an hour or less. Invite only the people necessary to special meetings, and confirm that they plan to attend in advance.

When practical, consider hijacking your regular team meeting agenda for some of your special-purpose meetings. Dispense with your normal team business quickly and move on to the particular topics. A primary purpose for a regular team meeting is to keep your staff connected, and for this any meaningful topic will suffice.

Strive for brevity. Encourage short meetings by moving topics not requiring live discussion to e-mail or other communications. (Especially status collection—no one needs to waste 15 minutes listening to endless variations of "Things are fine.") Set a formal agenda for every meeting that involves more than two people, and allocate time to each item you list. If your topic list is insufficient to fill the scheduled time, plan to end early. Distribute pre-meeting documents for review when possible to minimize the time you need to spend setting the context for discussion. To encourage meetings to end on time, and to avoid fragmenting productivity, schedule meetings to end at mealtime or at the end of the day.

Your meetings are not just for you. To be effective they must be for everyone. When inviting people to a meeting, look at the situation from their perspective. Do they need to be there? If not, don't invite them. Do they need to attend the whole meeting? If they don't, use your agenda to invite them to only the portions they need to see and manage the agenda so that when they join you will be on that topic. An alternative is to schedule more meetings, but invite only the people necessary to each. Although you will have more meetings, they will be shorter, and everyone else will have fewer and shorter meetings to deal with. Fine-tuning your meeting schedule to accomplish this depends on getting reliable commitments to attend from all who must be there, so confirm attendance with each person involved prior to the meeting.

Running Better Meetings

Effective meetings are well run. Start your meetings on time, and never be late to your own meetings. End early whenever possible, and don't end late. Use a "bucket list" to capture off-topic issues that arise, and don't let them lead discussions astray. Pick up any truly urgent topics listed at the end of the meeting if absolutely necessary (and if time allows), but follow up on all items listed after the meeting or on the agenda for a future meeting.

Set ground rules for regular meetings to establish norms for behavior and to set expectations that participants will not be wasting their time. After each meeting, take responsibility for summarizing all decisions and outcomes, and document and follow up on all action items generated. (Managing action items is covered in Problem 66.)

Dumping Unneeded Meetings

Before scheduling any meeting, consider if there might be a better way to accomplish the objectives. If there is, abort the meeting. Review all your current meetings and cancel all that are not necessary.

66. How can I ensure owner follow-through on project tasks and action items?

Getting things done starts with securing a meaningful commitment from an individual who will take responsibility for the work. Ideas for this are explored in Problem 48. Once you have agreement from an owner, effective execution depends on follow-through and closure of the project work, and for this you need to be proactive.

Following Up on Assignments

As your project proceeds, all scheduled work must commence, be attended to, and then be completed according to plan to keep the project on schedule. You must also drive the action items and other tasks found along the way to closure. To maximize the likelihood of all of this, you need to stay ahead of the game through reminders, inquiries during informal communications, and other means.

Status collection is central to this. In your weekly (or other periodic) requests for project status, list all the items of interest. In the status request you send to each contributor, include all of his or her assigned activities and action items that are coming due (plus any that are currently overdue) with relevant expected completion dates. Strive for meaningful interim status for any ongoing long-duration activities, not just "I'm doing fine." Also list any work scheduled to begin in the next two weeks, along with the expected start dates.

Be gentle but persistent regarding attention to due dates, especially early in your project. All due dates matter, and if you allow them to slip for early work it creates two potential problems. Time lost can never be recovered, so the few days you might put yourself behind in the first weeks of your project will ultimately result in either forced compression and extra stress for later work or a late project. The second problem is even more insidious. If you fail to manage due dates scrupulously at the beginning of your project, people will assume that they don't matter and will tend to pay little attention to them through the rest of the project.

If a task or an action item is overdue, or in serious danger of becoming overdue, approach the owner and explain the consequences of slippage. Discuss the impact it will have on the project, but focus on adverse effects that the individual particularly cares about.

Making Status Visible

Keep a list of open action items online as part of your project management information system (PMIS), and include for each a description, date opened, owner, current status, and due date. Quickly review action items in team meetings, focusing on those that are overdue or will be due before your next meeting. Call the owners of action items and project activities the day before they are due for a quick check-in, and as a reminder of the deadline.

If you are diligent and proactive, you can learn of problems and issues earlier and have more time and options for resolving them. If something must slip—because of a risk that is realized, an external dependency, an unexpected complexity, or any other reason—begin researching your options as soon as you learn of the problem. Get to work with your contributors and any others involved to revise your plans promptly. If you are considering changes that could affect work scheduled later in the project, involve the owners of that work in your replanning efforts too. Before committing to any plan adjustments, verify acceptance by everyone who will be affected. When you have determined what to do, update any relevant project documents and communicate the impact of the revisions to all stakeholders who need to know.

Include status of all current work in your weekly project reporting, including open action items. Make people aware that your reports will flag endangered items yellow and late items red, and use these flags consistently even when the activity owners are your managers. (But *always* warn everyone a few days in advance that this is coming, especially your managers, before doing it.) Circulate your status reports to all stakeholders who need to be informed, and promote the status of any significant late deliverables to the summary at the top of your written report.

As a last resort, escalate problems with overdue deadlines. Work with your sponsor, your management, your contributors' management, and others in authority to get things that are stalled back on track. Escalation is the thermonuclear option for dealing with project problems, because there will nearly always be permanent fallout and damaged relationships in its wake. If your project is important and there are no other viable options, however, escalation may be your only choice.

Closing Out Assignments

When the work is completed, update your documents to reflect it. When closed, mark action items "Done" in your PMIS and note their completion in your weekly status reporting. Update your tracking schedule to reflect closed tasks, and if the work was not completed on schedule— early *or* late—inform all of your team members who are affected.

67. How do I keep track of project details without things falling through the cracks?

Project leaders are always busy, so remaining on top of what is happening requires discipline and effective processes.

Tracking Dogmatically

Much of the job of a good project leader is effective communication. You must manage both inbound and outbound communications to ensure that you know what is going on and that all contributors and stakeholders have the information they need to do their jobs. Effective project monitoring starts with allocating sufficient time on your own calendar for it, so avoid overloading yourself with other duties that could make it impossible to keep up with your project.

Effective tracking is easiest when the granularity of the work is consistent with your communication and reporting cycles. A work breakdown structure containing work at the lowest level having two- to twenty-day durations—averaging about two weeks—will ensure that you will learn of most problems with sufficient lead time to deal with them. Following this guideline also avoids the unnecessary clutter of having to status hundreds of excessively short activities. As unplanned work is uncovered during your project, add it to your breakdown, and schedule and monitor that too.

As discussed in Problem 66, remaining proactive will provide needed advanced warning for problems, so always collect status updates from your contributors on work that is pending in addition to what is coming due. Gathering status on work scheduled to begin soon will permit you to better focus your overall efforts on keeping the project on track.

Being proactive also requires effective informal communications. In your conversations with your team members, ask what they are concerned about to uncover upcoming problems. Also discuss any current status issues, and explore any barriers, missing inputs, or other potential difficulties. Overall, strive to maintain good relationships and trust with all on your team, so that they will feel comfortable sharing what is really going on as it happens, even when it's not particularly good news.

Setting Up Effective Status Collection Processes

At the beginning of each project, set the frequency (generally weekly is best) that you will use for formal status collection. Get buy-in and agreement from each of your contributors to provide status on that basis, and start collection right from the start. Collect status every cycle, even when you are busy. In fact, it's especially important to collect status on a regular basis when things are busy and stressed. If you allow a problem in one area to distract you from what is happening in the rest of your project, other issues will arise without your knowledge and may well spin out of control before you even become aware of them.

If you are unable to collect status from a particular contributor, be persistent and follow up on the telephone, in person, or by other means. If you encounter chronic data collection problems, escalate as necessary to reinforce your need for progress information, and work to re-establish regular two-way status communication. When collecting project activity status, verify its accuracy using conversations and by participating in tests, evaluations, inspections, or other deliverable analysis.

Scheduling Periodic Reviews

Although weekly status collection is adequate for day-to-day project monitoring, you'll also need planning reviews to stay on top of projects with complicated life cycles or lengthy durations. Schedule reviews at life-cycle transitions, major project milestones, fiscal boundaries, or other times when a thorough reexamination of the project will be useful. For longer projects or programs, hold reviews at least every six months to stay within a realistic planning horizon. Use your reviews to update the activity lists, dependencies, and estimates, and to incorporate all newly discovered work into your plans. Update your requirements, risks, and other project information, modifying your project plans accordingly. Use the results of your reviews to get approval to proceed from your sponsor. Adjust your tracking and monitoring processes as appropriate to reflect any process improvements or other changes that result from your reviews.

If the review reveals the need for major changes, re-baseline your project with your sponsor and work with your stakeholders to manage their expectations.

68. How can I avoid having contributors game their status metrics?

Reliable project measurement is fundamental to effective tracking and monitoring. If the information you collect is flawed, you won't know what is happening, so you must establish an environment that encourages honest reporting and set up measures that align well with project objectives.

Establishing a Safe Reporting Environment

"Gaming" of metrics is what happens when people find ways to avoid providing information that reflects what is actually happening. When project metrics are gamed, you are working with flawed data. The most common root causes for inaccurate metrics relate to how they are used. When metrics are primarily used to detect and solve problems, people support them and cooperate. When metrics are used to find fault and punish, people provide them only grudgingly, and do whatever they can to provide results that demonstrate no problems—whether that's true or not. Gathering valid, useful information starts with a meaningful commitment on your part to use the measures for process improvement, good decision making, and project problem solving. If there is even a suspicion that data gathered will be used to criticize, punish, or even embarrass people, those responsible for reporting them will find a way to game the measures and disguise what is going on.

If you can ensure that all adverse status information that you collect will only be used to identify issues and focus attention and resources on their resolution, gaming of metrics will be rare. You must be scrupulous about maintaining this throughout your project, though. Even one counterexample can result in substantial mistrust and the prospect of largely unreliable future status.

One of the most effective means of sustaining open and honest status metric reporting is to involve the team members who will do the measurement in defining what needs to be measured and reported. Getting buy-in for measures where everyone is involved is a lot more straightforward than for the measures that are inflicted from outside or above. It also helps to approach each person involved, discuss the purpose and importance of the measures, and ask for him or her to agree to report the information on time and accurately to the best of his or her ability. People who have looked you in the eye and committed to not game their metrics are far less likely to provide erroneous information.

Also strive to verify accuracy and precision. Do what you can to ensure that the metrics you use may be easily confirmed, and at least spot-check them regularly to ensure their accuracy. If you detect a problem, follow up promptly and work with those collecting the data to ensure accurate future data. If you need to confront contributors regarding a measurement issue, do it one-on-one, and let them participate in any recommendations for fixing the problem.

Another important data reliability factor relates to how visible the metrics will be. If you are collecting potentially personal information, commit to keeping it private. Examples of such data include adverse performance or attendance data that reveals information that the members of your team would prefer not be public. If you need to collect such information, never report it except in aggregate for the whole team so that it will not be obvious who is involved—or better yet, don't report it publically at all. Ensure that any follow-up discussion regarding private information is strictly between you and the person involved. (There is one big exception to this, however. If you find yourself wandering into potentially dangerous legal territory, get help. When you become aware of anything that crosses the line into inappropriate, unethical, illegal, or other behavior that violates your organizational policies, immediately involve your management, your human resources specialists, or others who know what they are doing. Let the pros take this over; this is not your job as a project leader.)

Aligning Metrics and Goals

Useful information also depends on clear definition. Thoroughly describe each project metric you intend to collect so that each person responsible for collecting it knows exactly what is to be measured, and how. Metric definitions include what you are measuring, how it is to be used, how it is to be derived, frequency, units for reporting, and other factors. If several people are asked to provide the same metric and there is a good definition, you can expect consistent measures, not a wide range of results.

Metrics work best when they directly relate to stated goals and expected behaviors. Before adding any particular metric to your status collection and reporting, determine how it relates to the ultimate success of your project. If a specific metric has only a tenuous connection to what you are trying to accomplish, drop it.

You will also get better results when your metrics are in balance. For example, having only a metric for speed or only a metric for accuracy won't help your project very much. If you measure only speed, your deliverable might work poorly. If you measure only accuracy, you may never finish. Metrics for both used together, though, will create tension and provide the balance your project needs to deal with trade-offs and best achieve your goals.

69. What are the best ways to communicate project status?

Project status–reporting problems fall into two categories: There's too much of it, or there's too little. Striking an appropriate balance is not difficult, but it does take a bit of effort.

Reporting Regular Status

Your main objective in project status reporting is to provide the information people need while keeping your communications overhead under control. If you provide reports to lots of people, the overhead can be overwhelming. It's best to craft a format that can be easily edited to serve multiple audiences, so you do not get stuck writing a dozen different reports every week. One technique that serves this end is to use the "inverted pyramid" style of writing employed by newspapers. The most relevant and important information is up front, in the headlines and first paragraph or two. Additional information may follow, but each succeeding portion is less important than what came before.

Applying this idea to a weekly (or other periodic) project status report is not difficult. Start each report with a set of "headlines," three to five bullets that summarize what is most important about your project since your last status report. Include in this executive summary any significant accomplishments, issues you are working on, and major work that's pending. Use your summary to name contributors with noteworthy recent accomplishments to recognize and keep them motivated.

Follow your summary with more detailed information on activities, timing, costs, issues, action items, and other project details, sequenced according to relative importance. For your team, the entire report will probably be relevant. For project leaders of related projects and some of your stakeholders, the first half may be of interest. For your sponsor, your management, and the rest of your stakeholders, it could be that only the executive summary will be necessary. Starting the report with a clear summary helps everyone understand what's most important, and customizing by chopping off trailing portions of the report lets you tailor it for different readers without killing yourself.

The leading summary is most important, so work to focus it on the most relevant information and choose your words carefully to convey the message you need people to hear. The remainder of the report matters as well, but it will always have a lot less impact than the first few lines (and that's all that many people will read anyway). Especially in the summary and other up-front sections, exclude trivia and information that is well known or self-evident. Report on the things that matter most to the community surrounding your project, including details on any changes to scope, risks, issues, activities, or any other relevant project information.

The worst status reports say little more than "We are doing okay," and provide no analysis or specific details. Although this kind of reporting may be tempting to harried project leaders with too much to do, it will cause your sponsor and stakeholders to lose confidence. It also communicates to your team that you don't care about details, and they will soon stop providing any themselves. If you expect your contributors to supply accurate timely status, you'll need to set an example by doing the same, and include what they provide so each team member can see that their inputs are being used.

Also not useful are reports created by lazy project leaders who collect status write-ups from each contributor and simply concatenate them in random order into a humongous string of text with no organization. Although this style of report may include all relevant information, somewhere, no one will be able to find it and few will even try.

You also need to keep your project management information system current. Drop a copy of your periodic project status report where people can find it along with earlier versions. Use the status you collect to update lists, action items, tracking schedules, and other planning documents in your archive, so contributors can find and use up-to-date information to guide their work.

Preparing Special Reports

In addition to regular weekly reporting, you will probably need to prepare less frequent, high-level reports. This sort of reporting is often coincident with project reviews, life-cycle phase transitions, fiscal period ends, or specific management requests. These reports tend to take a longer view, and focus on both what has been accomplished to date and what is planned for the future. Although there may be less detail in these reports, the audience for such reporting (and often a formal presentation) will be your management, sponsor, and key stakeholders. You will need to be clear and crisp, and focus on the positives.

You may get few opportunities to communicate what you are doing and how you are progressing to your management, so take full advantage of these reports to build continuing support and interest in your project.

Another special case is your final project report. As your project wraps up, document what your overall project has accomplished. Summarize your results, and emphasize the goals you met and the value and benefits you have delivered. Include specifics on people and teams who did the work, and recognize their contributions. A final report is also a great opportunity to raise issues that emerged in your post-project retrospective analysis—using your lessons learned to propose changes and improvements that will make future projects more successful.

70. How can I manage my project successfully despite high-priority interruptions?

In a perfect world, projects would exist in their own hermetically sealed environment and things could proceed without interruption through to a successful closure. In the real world, stuff happens and we need to deal with it through prioritization, and when necessary, replanning.

Prioritizing Work

When a project leader gets a request to work on something outside the project, there are several possibilities. To determine which will be most appropriate, begin by assessing relative priorities. If your project is strategic and considered vital by your management, you might get away with "Sorry, I can't be spared to help you," or "I'd love to help you later, but not right now." You will likely need to deal with interruptions that appear to be more important than your project, though.

Before abandoning your project, at least get a sense of how much time and effort the request will require, and inform your sponsor and key stakeholders about any consequences of your absence. This may shift the relative priorities, and in some cases your sponsor's reaction might even result in the person with the hot request deciding to seek help elsewhere.

Managing Your Absence

You'll need to manage around any interruptions that do take you away from your project. If the amount of time and effort needed from you is small, this may have only minor consequences for your project. Good project leaders strive not to overbook their own time, so you probably have a small amount of reserve to work with. Any slack time you manage to retain in your schedule is there for dealing with risks and other situations that arise in your own project, but for small requests this could potentially be diverted to help out externally. Also, you probably have at least one person on your team who can pick up critical project leadership responsibilities in your absence—usually the same contributor you would rely upon when you are ill, on vacation, or otherwise unavailable. The reality is that for small high-priority requests, the answer for most of us will not be entirely satisfactory, but it boils down to "Deal with it."

For requests that are bigger, representing significantly more than a week or so of your time, there will almost certainly be a noticeable impact on your project. In these cases, document the specific consequences for your project, and discuss them with your sponsor. If a suitable project leader can be identified to fill in for you while you are focused on outside work, arrange to make the job for your temporary replacement as seamless as possible.

If no one is available to substitute for you and your absence will substantially affect your project, use your data to adjust your stakeholder expectations to be in line with what can realistically be delivered. Replan your project to reflect your temporary absence, and get approval to reset your project baseline.

71. What are the best project management communication techniques for remote contributors?

Effective communication with remote team members starts with establishing relationships and trust, as discussed in Problem 39. Building on a solid teamwork foundation, you can draw from a variety of useful techniques and ideas.

Communicating Informally

Maintaining effective teamwork starts with your one-on-one relationship with each member of your team. Take full advantage of all opportunities to visit face-to-face with all of your remote contributors, whether you travel to visit them or you bring them to visit with you. This takes time and costs money, but the alternative—disconnection and potential conflicts—will nearly always be worse. If possible, find a way to meet in person with each member of your team at least twice per year.

Also take advantage when others travel. Discover contacts that you have in common and set up short meetings involving them to reinforce your connections when they are visiting a site where you have a team member (or if they work with someone on your team, to meet with you when in town). Travelers are also a good, personal way to deliver small things to distant contributors, such as small project rewards, team T-shirts, and the like.

Practice "tele-MBWA," using communications tools to "manage by wandering around" with those who are not nearby. Call people who are far away a few times a month "just to talk," without any formal agenda or question in mind. You will find more discussion on MBWA and other informal communications with team members who are far away in Problem 44.

Informal communications also include e-mail and other electronic messaging. Take advantage of opportunities to share pictures and information of interest that has nothing to do with your project. Strive to keep in contact, and work to make people who are far away feel they are part of your team.

Communicating Formally

Between the opportunities that you have to interact face-to-face, take full advantage of all available communications technologies. Make use of audio- and videoconferencing as frequently as practical, and justify using the best capabilities you can find. There is more on the topic of tools for global communications and networking in Problems 72 and 96. Schedule time to interact one-on-one at least weekly with each member of your project team. You can significantly increase the effectiveness of these calls if you schedule them during your contributor's normal workday, even if this is not convenient for you. Formal meetings are another aspect of projects that can work either for or against you with remote contributors. Make all your project meetings as efficient and short as practical, and ensure that the timing is as acceptable to everyone as possible. Meet early in the morning or late in the evening, at least part of the time, to fairly spread the pain and loss of sleep around to all. Make remote participation in your meetings easy for everyone, providing network connections or pre-meeting distribution of all visual materials to be discussed. Be sensitive to the length of meetings where people are participating via telephone where much more than an hour will likely result in loss of interest and involvement.

Set up your weekly status requests to make responding to them as easy as possible for your distant team members. If you are dealing with several native languages, ensure that written information you send out is clearly and unambiguously understood by all. If necessary, provide translations of reports and important project documents.

Follow up any telephone calls and meetings where you have discussed complex matters with an e-mail summarizing what was covered so your remote team members can review it in detail. Also follow up complex documents that you distribute with a telephone call so you can discuss the material and allow your remote staff to ask any questions. By and large, strive to "overcommunicate." With remote team members there is a natural inclination toward "out of sight, out of mind," so project leaders rarely invest enough time with distant contributors. Doing more than you think is necessary might just be barely enough.

72. How do I establish effective global communications? What metrics can I use to track communications?

Some of the purposes served by remote communications are explored in Problem 71, along with some ideas for making them more effective. Discussion of project communications tools can be found in Problem 96. This problem focuses primarily on how best to communicate globally.

Using Telecommunications

There are many tools for audio teleconferencing, and most of us these days use them extensively and relatively well. If you plan to use speakerphone equipment, check that it is in good working order and is of high enough quality to ensure that those who are not in the same room with the speakerphone will be able to understand everything that's said, even from the corners of the room far from the microphones. There may also be sound quality issues when including mobile phone or "Web phone" users in teleconferences. If background noise or distortion causes problems, work to ensure more reliable connections for affected participants at future meetings.

Also take advantage of Web-enabled computer display sharing for remote meetings. Check all equipment settings to ensure compatibility, and choose a networking application that's suitable for your meeting needs. Use dynamic "network meeting place" software for small meetings, and "Webinar" applications to present to large, distributed groups. Whatever type of Web-sharing software you use, provide an effective way for all to negotiate past any relevant security or firewalls.

Videoconferencing is also becoming a lot more popular, and it's a great way to share complex information and to show the faces of remote meeting participants. If you plan to take advantage of video gear or special rooms for your meetings, ensure that all the setups are compatible and that you have budgeted for any ongoing expense associated with using specialized facilities. In some cases, the inconvenience of coming to a special room and the complexity of connecting the video setups may exceed the value of videoconferencing. If so, consider more convenient audio options along with Web sharing to realize many of the same advantages. In all cases, use the best and most effective communications tools that are available to everyone on your team for your meetings.

There are also countless other ways to connect one-on-one to others these days, starting with various types of instant and text messaging, and including all the variations of "social networking." Trendy project leaders tap into as much of this as their team members desire to (or will tolerate), and any of these means can provide powerful support for reinforcing trust and building strong interpersonal relationships. Consider issues of organizational policy, security, and technological compatibility in adopting these kinds of dynamic technological communications. If they meet your organization's guidelines and help you stay in touch with your team, take full advantage of them.

Remember that for many of your important project communications you need to ensure that there is a permanent record. In these cases, continue to rely on (or at least follow up with) regular e-mail or other messaging that provides an audit trail.

Setting Up a Global PMIS

Global teams have special requirements for their project management information system (PMIS). Many considerations for establishing a PMIS are discussed in Problem 33. As part of your PMIS for a global team, ensure that you are making plans, issue lists, change logs, and other project documents fully available around the clock. Set up PMIS access so that it's open to all who need it, but secured against those who don't. If you have links in your PMIS to information stored in other locations, check that all of your team members have full access to the other file shares, Web sites, and any other places referenced by such links. Implementing your PMIS with "knowledge management" software that provides search capabilities will increase its utility. Such applications can also improve your control of the PMIS by letting you establish alerts to advise you when anyone modifies critical project information.

Strive to ensure that all of your team members have acceptable response time for information access, including those who are far away. If necessary, consider using synchronized "mirror" sites on distributed servers to better support your distant staff.

Measuring Global Communications

There are many potentially beneficial communications metrics for distributed team communications. A few that may be most useful include:

▲ Status responses on first or subsequent requests
▲ Counts of inbound and outbound messages
▲ Access statistics for your online PMIS
▲ Issue aging and counts
▲ Frequency of requests that you receive to provide information available online

If you detect data patterns that reveal a lack of two-way communication or lack of engagement (either by contributor or by location), investigate why. Work with your team to improve participation.

73. On fee-for-service projects, how do I balance customer and organizational priorities?

When you agree to manage projects on a contract basis, you are signing up to serve two masters. You may need to walk a tightrope to keep both your own organization's management and your paying customer happy. Managing trade-offs in such situations begins with identifying any lack of alignment, and then taking action to minimize and manage potential conflicts.

Understanding Potential Differences

In the bid phase of a fee-for-service project, carefully analyze the customer requirements in relationship to your organization's strategies and expertise. There are many reasons to decline an opportunity to bid for work, starting with whether the job is a good fit with what you do well. After considerations of competence, the next hurdle will generally concern whether the potential project is something that you want to get involved with. Some "no bid" decisions are based on size—a particular job may be too big, or perhaps even too small.

Other things to consider include longer-term benefits such as the potential for follow-on business and the value of the project or customer relationship for reference purposes. Also think about any aspects of the potential relationship that may be undesirable for some reason. If there are obvious differences between the stated core organizational principles and those of a potential customer, they may be a compelling reason to pass up the bid opportunity. The oft-quoted principle at Google, "Don't be evil," is an example of a core belief that could guide decisions to embrace some opportunities and to run away screaming from others. If a project opportunity carries potential conflicts involving issues of ethics, business values, or even political philosophy, avoiding a contract relationship in the first place is probably your best option. (Not all such differences may be apparent early in the bidding, contracting, and initiation phases for the work. Some philosophical conflicts may arise later, despite your diligent evaluation of the opportunity at hand.)

Most other conflicts common in fee-for-service projects come down to changes and costs. Your best defense for these is to spend sufficient time analyzing the "request for proposal" to develop the precise understanding of the performance and other deliverable requirements you will need to develop your response. If some feature or aspect of the desired scope is unclear, follow up to investigate exactly what is needed before crafting your bid.

For any work you plan to pursue, analyze any potential differences in priority or other conflicts between your organization and your prospective customer. If you do decide to respond, explicitly deal with potential conflicts by incorporating language in your proposal. Describe any specific constraints regarding what processes you plan to use, any standards you will apply, and any other significant things that you will or will not do as part of the project. Within your organization, determine how to price the work to be in line with your assessment of the risks you will carry, your goals for profit, and any other financial considerations important to your management.

Negotiating the Contract

Effectively dealing with conflicts later in the project starts with setting the contract terms. Ensure that the contract includes clear, unambiguous language describing all deliverables, with measurable criteria regarding acceptance. Also incorporate language describing the process and consequences of any changes to the project or the deliverable, including how to document changes, who will approve them, and the precise impact any accepted changes will have on pricing and other contract terms. If you included specific exclusions or any other constraints in your proposal, see that they are incorporated into the contract. Anything that causes problems later that is not explicitly covered in the contract will generally be resolved in favor of your customer's priorities. If something matters to you and your organization, ensure that it's included in the contract that you sign. If you don't, you may end up absorbing the consequences later, whether you want to or not.

Managing Conflicts

During a fee-for-service project, the main operating principle tends to be "The customer is always right." As your project proceeds, you must work for a hierarchy of sponsors. For most matters, the dominant voice will be the customer who engaged you to do the work. The opinions of your sponsor/manager in your own organization are secondary, because your customer controls whether you get paid, and that is ultimately your organization's primary stake in the project.

Whenever conflicts with your customer arise, consult the contract to see if it offers any support for your position. If the contract terms clearly support your interpretation, take a firm stand. Let your customer decide whether to back down or to renegotiate to change the contract to get what he or she desires.

If your contract offers no help, you will probably need to comply with your customer's position. If this means changing what you are doing, or redoing work you have already completed, your organization may have to eat the costs and deal with any other consequences this entails. In general, your top priority throughout your project will be maintaining your customer's satisfaction, while managing the expectations of all your other stakeholders the best you are able.

In some extreme cases, you may encounter conflicts that are sufficiently severe that you'll consider abandoning the project altogether, or at least taking a firm position contrary to your customer's wishes. Before doing anything overt, discuss the situation with your own management and clearly consider all the potential negative consequences, costs, and legal ramifications. In most situations such as this, you will probably decide to hunker down and work through the conflicts and difficulties to put the whole project behind you (and to resolve not to get into similar situations in the future). There may be times, however, when your management concludes that tearing up a contract and walking away will be the best way to minimize its losses.

Again, avoiding projects in the first place that have potential for conflict and committing only to work that has adequate protections included in the contract terms are your best defenses against getting caught in cross-organizational strife.

74. How do I survive a late-project work bulge, ensuring both project completion and team cohesion?

We've all been here. The deadline looms and an enormous amount of work remains. If your deadline can't move, it's best to see problems in advance so you can explore options such as modifying your scope or applying more resources. Regardless of how you proceed, you may bruise some relationships. But by managing well, you can minimize the impact.

Anticipating Problems

As you plan your projects, spend some time reviewing past similar work where the last few weeks were stressful and chaotic. Looking at your past projects, what might you do differently? What recommendations emerged from the lessons learned for projects led by others? How could you run your current project differently to ensure a more coherent end game?

If past projects have gotten into trouble due to weak scoping definition, focus more effort on requirement planning, discussed in Problem 22. If excessive changes, particularly late in the project, have caused problems, revisit your change management process (covered in Problem 84), and set earlier limitations on when changes can be considered. If past testing issues are a result of insufficient early specifications, define concrete activities early in your project to nail down testing and evaluation criteria. Overall, seek to set up your project to avoid things that have caused past difficulties.

Also focus on project risks, especially risks that relate to testing, acceptance, and other late-project work. Develop contingency plans to help you deal with unanticipated work near the end of your project. Consider options for getting outsourced help or "borrowing" staff from other projects, expediting techniques that could compress work durations, using potential "shortcuts," and moving staff off-site to reduce distractions and interruptions. Include budget reserve in your project plans, based on the estimated costs of your contingency plans and metrics from past projects. If your risk analysis reveals significant probable delays, also negotiate a due date that includes an adequate schedule reserve.

Schedule periodic reviews on projects with durations longer than about six months. Use your reviews to assess progress, and set expectations that adjustments to the timing objectives may be necessary as a result of the reviews. If significant changes prove necessary, begin discussions and negotiations as early as you can; never wait until the last minute to begin admitting you have problems.

Getting the Project Done

If you are up against an immovable deadline that is close and there is more work remaining than you can realistically complete with your current team as planned, start considering changes. The easiest changes to make in the short term tend to be to your team members' work schedules. Consider the effect of dropping any other responsibilities outside of the project for the remainder of your schedule to focus more time and effort on project tasks. If overtime is an option, consider that, too (but this may only solve one problem by creating another). When there is more work to do than a realistic schedule permits, you may need to be creative. Investigate to see if there might be any viable options for delivering on time through extra staffing or contract help, or some other expediting technique.

If you still face timing problems, reexamine your project's requirements to see if dropping some of them could help. Begin with your lowest-priority specifications, and investigate if removing any of them could make enough of a difference. Before proposing any changes to your scope, compare the value of the requirements you might drop with any estimated costs of the additional resource costs required to keep them. If paying for the additional help can be justified, plan to propose that instead.

Work to reconcile the realities of the "iron triangle" of scope, schedule, and cost for the remainder of your project, trading off between scope revisions and additional resources as needed to protect the schedule with the least overall impact.

Retaining Friends

It is often possible to get a project done on time through a combination of superhuman effort and somewhat diminished scope. Doing this without some emotional cost is unlikely, but good project leaders work hard to minimize the pain and damage to long-term relationships. This often starts with sacrifices that you will need to make. You need to show that you are willing to do at least as much yourself as you are asking of others. Plan to take on administrative burdens for others to free up more of their time. If people are working late, weekends, and holidays, plan to be there too. Pitch in with work where you are qualified. Even if you are not able to directly contribute, do what you can to facilitate progress, such as running for food, handling follow-up and communications tasks, and other efforts that will help. Be encouraging and appreciative, and remain upbeat. Shorten or eliminate meetings where practical, and personally deal with any extra work that this might mean for you without complaining.

Also keep overall track of where any extra burdens are falling and work to balance the load across your team. Encourage people to help each other. If everyone feels that all are in this together in times of stress, collaboration can increase teamwork and build stronger relationships. Intervene quickly to defuse any conflicts or arguments, and do the best you can to maintain peace. Energy spent fighting will only make your project work bulge bigger.

75. How do I coordinate improvements and changes to processes we are currently using on our project?

If you realize in the midst of a project that you have a process problem, you should consider fixing it. Before embarking on a process improvement effort during execution, you need to consider the overall impact on the project. If the potential long-term benefits are significant, though, it may be better to act sooner than later.

Assessing the Need for Change

If you are having difficulty during your project with any of your processes or methods, work with your team to assess potential improvements. Develop documentation for both your current "as is" process and a more desirable "to be" process. Verify the performance of the current process using project status information, and set measurable, specific improvement goals for the new version. In some situations, the needed changes may be obvious and take little effort to analyze. If getting diverted into this will materially affect your project, however, you'll need to justify the effort to your sponsor before going too far. If improving your process could adversely affect the project objective, it may be better to meet your current project's commitments and then deal with process improvement afterward.

If you can realistically integrate a process change into your project within its constraints, proceed with your process planning. If the process affects only you, determine the costs and benefits of making the change and proceed. If the change could affect others, involve them in your analysis. For processes that do affect others, involve them in your planning or at least enlist their support to conduct a pilot for a revised process on your project that they might later adopt.

Planning for Change

Develop a process description for the new process, and document its operating procedures. Develop any training materials or job aids needed

189

for implementation, and adjust any project estimates that will be shortened or lengthened by the new process.

Enlist the participation of those who will be directly involved in the new process planning for the change, and get their buy-in. Work to gain the support of any other process stakeholders who will not be directly involved, using vivid descriptions of the benefits of the improvements and credibly documented measurable results.

If the process will affect your project objective or have impact beyond your immediate team, also solicit the support of your sponsor and management before proceeding.

Making and Managing the Change

Use training, mentoring, and process guidance to implement the process change for your project. Monitor the results obtained using the revised process, and compare them with your improvement goals. Also look for unintended consequences and other adverse effects. If your revised process fails to work as planned, work to correct it by adjusting the process definition (or execution). If your new process proves to be ineffective following your attempts to fix it, back it out and return to using the earlier process.

If your process change does achieve your expected performance goals, however, adopt it permanently as part of your standard project management practices.

76. How much project documentation is enough?

Depends on:
▲ Project type and size
▲ Legal requirements
▲ Organizational and other standards
▲ Relevant methodologies

Defining Documentation Needs

All projects require some level of documentation. Large projects need a lot of documents because of their complexity and to serve the needs of a big team. Tiny projects may need very little, perhaps only some handwritten lists of things to do and to verify. At a minimum, every project must at least meet the documentation standards mandated by the organization, and may also need documents required by regulatory requirements, industry standards, and methodology needs. (Problem 6 explores some considerations related to standards and methodologies.) Determining exactly what is useful to include beyond the minimum required for your organization is up to your judgment, but what follows includes some typical project-specific and general documentation.

Specifying Project Documents

Most project documents relate to definition, planning, or status. For sizable projects, most documentation will be stored in an online project management information system (discussed in Problem 33), where all team members can access it any time and from anywhere.

Definition documents will usually include:

▲ Project charter and overall project definition
▲ Deliverable requirements (including priorities, measurable specifications, and evaluation criteria)
▲ Team roster (with roles and contact information)

▲ Stakeholder analysis
▲ Contracts and other agreements

Planning information will typically contain, at least:

▲ Project work breakdown structure dictionary
▲ Project schedule
▲ Resource analysis and plans
▲ Risk register
▲ Specific plans as needed, such as communications, quality, or procurement

Status information will evolve as the project progresses, and normally will consist of a sequence of versions of:

▲ Status reports
▲ Change logs
▲ Issue-tracking logs
▲ Life-cycle and other reviews
▲ Project presentations
▲ Testing results
▲ Meeting minutes
▲ Formal communications

Specifying General Documents

In addition to documents describing your specific project, you will likely need some documentation for your overall processes and methods. These include such items as:

▲ Specification change process
▲ Testing standards
▲ Methodology and standards definitions
▲ Configuration control procedures
▲ Project infrastructure decisions and practices

Every project is different, so there can be enormous variation from project to project for the documentation necessary in any of these categories. What you judge to be necessary could be a lot more, or a lot less, than what is listed here.

77. How can I ensure all members on my multi-site team have all the information they need to do their work?

For project teams that are not located together there can be major problems with synchronization and information access. Effective project leaders work to ensure that everyone has access to the same information throughout the project.

Managing Communications

Keeping everyone on a distributed team in sync is the responsibility of the project leader. Effectively communicating with remote team members is explored in Problem 71. Project communication requires both formal reports and team meetings and periodic informal conversations.

Use your one-on-one meetings and informal conversations to enhance your ongoing control. Invite questions from your remote contributors, and ask about any current problems they are having. Also discuss upcoming challenges, risks, and potential conflicts to get a sense of what each of your team members thinks will happen in the near future. Talk about plans for current and scheduled activities, and work to resolve any differences if you detect anything that is not consistent with your overall plans.

When there are substantial changes that affect the project, set up a specific meeting with your whole team to discuss them. Provide explicit written documentation that clearly describes how the changes will affect each person's work. Follow up individually with each of your contributors to ensure that all your team members understand the impact of the changes on them. Also walk through any updated project documents and ensure that no one continues to use obsolete versions for their work.

Maintaining Your Project Management Information System

A thorough, well-organized information base is the foundation for coordinating a distributed project team. Establishing an online project management information system (PMIS) is discussed in Problem 33, and Problem 72 includes some pointers about using it to supplement global communications. When establishing it, work to ensure adequate access for all of your team members, regardless of their locations. Emphasize that the current versions of all project documents and plans will be stored online in your PMIS, and discourage use of offline copies that might not be up-to-date. When you distribute reports or other communications, provide links to the main documents in your online repository, not attachments.

When communicating changes, verify that the primary versions of all documents are the most easily found, and that earlier versions are stored in a way that makes access more difficult (for example, in an archive folder or accessible only through an automated push-down function for retrieving previous versions). When discussing updated documents following a project change with each of your contributors, ask them to delete any earlier local copies of revised documents and emphasize the locations of the principal versions online in the PMIS.

78. How can I manage overly constrained projects effectively?

Depends on:
▲ Project value
▲ Project priority

Managing Constraints

All projects have constraints. The deadline sets a time constraint. Your finite list of assigned contributors sets a firm staffing constraint, and also limits your budget. For some projects these constraints may be soft, where the consequences of failing to meet one or both are not a big deal. For other projects they may be immovable. What is always true, however, is that for any particular project only some combinations of scope, time, and cost are possible. The top-down objectives for a project may start out as completely reasonable, absolutely impossible, or anywhere in between. If your process for setting a project baseline fails to drive the initial top-down goals into consistency with your plan-based, bottom-up analysis, your project will not succeed. If your initial project objectives are unrealistic, you must adjust them.

To do this, you will need to use your planning data to negotiate a more plausible set of objectives with your sponsor and stakeholders. This process starts with verifying the overall constraints provided by your sponsor and key stakeholders in their initial top-down objectives. Plan to ask "Why?" a lot, and probe persistently to uncover the basis for each starting assumption. In your discussions with your sponsor, determine which of time, scope, or cost is most important. Don't accept "All three" as an answer. Get a sense of which of the factors is most consequential by devising scenario-based questions. Ask questions such as: "Would it be better to be a week late or to spend a bit more money on a contractor to help us meet the deadline?" Keep digging until you know which constraints are truly constrained and which are most negotiable. (It's never credible to constrain all three initially, as is implicit in the old saying: "Fast, good, cheap. Pick two."). Planning is your next step. Avoid committing to any firm project objectives before you have developed a good sense of what is possible.

Understanding the Work

Collaborate with your team in developing a credible, bottom-up plan that can realistically deliver all scoping requirements. (Effectively dealing with planning challenges is explored earlier in this book, in Problems 48 through 64.) For your initial plans, let the project duration and cost factors fall wherever they may; focus on defining, estimating, and sequencing all the work necessary to create your deliverable. If your project is particularly risky, also incorporate provisions for contingencies and reserve in your plans.

There will likely be significant differences between your initial plans and at least some of your sponsor's original goals. If so, attempt to adjust your plan so that it meets the highest priority among scope, time, and cost. If the best plan you can devise remains inconsistent with your primary objective, attempt to optimize it using techniques such as rearranging dependencies, shortening durations through staffing changes, or using other means. If your best plan version is still well outside the original goals, create several additional plan variations that come as close as possible to meeting the stated objectives for just scope, time, or cost alone, or in pairs.

Especially in cases where the differences are particularly extreme, engage your team in exploring opportunities. Seek ways to deliver better results (perhaps by employing an emerging technology that your stakeholders are not aware of). Redefine the project deliverable so it solves a class of problems instead of only the particular one it's aimed at. Segment the work to deliver some useful functionality much earlier and the full requested deliverable in later phases. In general, brainstorm other project variations that might represent superior business opportunities. (At times when you know that you are going to lose an argument, the best strategy may be to change the subject.)

Prepare for discussion with your sponsor by making summaries of plans for alternative projects that can realistically be undertaken. Your planning data provides the fact-based information you'll need to conduct a principled negotiation with your sponsor and stakeholders. Use the data to negotiate a credible baseline for your project.

Negotiating a Realistic Baseline

Meet with your sponsor to discuss the project and set your baseline for project tracking and control. Start your discussion with a summary of your best plan version (even if it is at significant variance with the initial project goals). Demonstrate that it is consistent with past similar projects and is based on thorough analysis. If your primary plan significantly differs from the original request, also present your additional plan-based project alternatives as other options.

Discuss the value of the project, and discuss the resource requirements in your plan in contrast with the expected benefits. Also explore the project's overall priority, and any relationship between that and the duration shown in your plan. Focus your discussions on comparing your project's plan-based needs with its expected results, not with arbitrarily determined time or cost constraints.

If you encounter resistance, discuss the potential consequences of setting an unrealistic baseline. No one wins with a project that has an impossible goal. You lose because your project fails. Your team loses because it will have been involved with an unsuccessful, depressing experience. Even your sponsor and management lose when they force acceptance of an unrealizable objective. They initiated the project, and presumably they need what it is expected to produce. If it fails, they won't have what they want either.

Principled negotiation is based on facts and data, which are your only real advantages in project negotiations. The other parties may be more persuasive and certainly have more organizational power than you do. Fortunately for you, there is also power in knowledge, and that's on your side. After planning your project, you are the world's leading authority on it. (And, your experience and knowledge were why you were asked to lead the project in the first place.) In negotiating to adjust unrealistic constraints, you must use what you know.

Resist emotional plays to flatter you, such as, "You are the best project leader we have. Surely you can do this!" It really does not matter how talented you are if the project cannot be done. If you are faced with demands to finish the project faster, hold up your project schedule showing the minimum duration with all its red and blue bars. Ask your sponsor to pick any activities you should drop to meet a shorter deadline. This is a very effective way to show that a shorter project is infeasible, and most managers back down quickly.

With solid evidence of what is and is not possible, you should be able to engage your sponsors and stakeholders in collaborative problem solving instead of posturing. Discuss with them any alternate project plans you have developed, and work together to find a version of the project that is both possible and a good business proposition. If you have identified any promising opportunities, discuss them as well and explore if they would be worth pursuing.

Work to establish a baseline for your project where the overall constraints are consistent with a credible set of plans, including a sufficient reserve (budget and/or schedule) to deal with the overall project risk.

79. How do I keep my project from slipping? If it does, how do I recover its schedule?

Managing schedule performance starts with proactive tracking and requires quick response for any adverse variances.

Monitoring Schedule Variance

When you collect status on your current work (generally weekly), also request information on work scheduled to begin in the next two weeks. Encourage your team members to inform you as soon as they know of any potential problems with required inputs, initiation, execution, or completion of all current and imminent work for which they are responsible. Also request that your contributors let you know about needed work that was missed in earlier planning.

Use your informal conversations with project staff members to discuss things that could affect upcoming work, and talk about their current and future concerns about the project. Keep alert for anything that could affect your timeline, including systems outages, predicted severe weather, or other external factors. Also, periodically review your project risks and use your analysis as an early warning for potential schedule slips.

Work to detect scheduling problems as early as possible, and deal with them when they are small. The longer it takes for you to notice them, the harder you will have to work to recover and the fewer options you will have for doing so.

Managing Your Critical Path

If there are any delays (or projected delays) affecting critical project activities that could impact your deadline, determine the magnitude of the slip. If the slip is minor, recover using small amounts of overtime or getting help from within your team to expedite activities and catch up. In some cases, successor activities may be able to begin on time (per-

haps with some small risk), even if all the prior work is not quite finished.

For more significant delays, begin recovery by using any contingency that you may have set up to deal with that specific problem in
your risk planning or by applying overall reserves in time or money that
you have established at the project level. Investigate the possibilities
for revising some dependencies to allow subsequent work to begin on
schedule, restaffing upcoming work to reduce critical task estimates, or
"crashing" future work in your project by adding additional resources
to get you back on track.

As a last resort, escalate particularly severe slips that you cannot
resolve within your project to your sponsor. If your schedule problem
is sufficiently serious, you may need to propose revising your project
baseline (or even cancelling the project).

Communicating Your Status

Managing schedule problems also requires effective, honest communication. For each significant issue you are managing, include a note in
your summary at the head of your next status report describing your
schedule problem. Include specifics about what you have done or are
doing about it, and follow up with updates in all subsequent reports
until you have resolved your scheduling issue.

80. What are the best practices for managing schedule changes?

Depends on:

▲ Project scale
▲ Project priorities
▲ The cause for the change

Analyzing the Need for Change

The focus of this problem is schedule changes to pull in a deadline. (Managing schedule slippage is discussed in Problem 79.) Demands for schedule compression generally result from either solving project problems or requests from a customer or other stakeholder. Solving a problem is generally urgent, so the sooner you start to make the changes, the better off you will be. Requested changes are usually discretionary, so the best response at least some of the time is to say "no." Whether or not to make a schedule change comes down to a business decision: Will your project be better off having made a change, or would it make more sense to leave things as they are? Whatever the motivation, when considering a scheduling change, make a decision about it promptly.

As with any project change decision, the primary considerations are cost and benefits. The cost of a schedule change can vary a great deal, depending on exactly how it is to be done. Use "what if?" planning to explore options and develop cost estimates. Consider tactics such as revising activity dependencies, expediting or "crashing" work remaining through extra funding, increasing the project staff by reassigning people from other work or hiring outside contractors, reducing schedule reserve (if you have any), and any other schedule compression ideas you can come up with. For small requested schedule changes, rearranging the remaining work and adding a little overtime may be sufficient. For larger changes, seek a combination of viable tactics that will shorten your project with a minimum of additional cost and increased risk. Where appropriate, also investigate possible scoping reductions that may be necessitated by the schedule change, and estimate any associated opportunity costs.

The decision also requires assessing what the change will be worth, so also estimate the value of any expected benefits from the change. In cases where you must respond to a competitor's announcement to protect any project value, the benefits may be substantial and easy to verify. For most cases, though, be skeptical of the purported benefits of the schedule reduction and request information on how they were estimated. If the cost of compressing the schedule is small and the benefits are large, work with your sponsor and stakeholders to make a sound business decision on how to proceed. If the benefits are small, or questionable, compared with the costs and risks, strongly resist moving in your deadline.

Adopting a Schedule Change

If you intend to commit to a shorter schedule, work to revise your planning documents. Revise your activity cost and duration estimates as appropriate, noting all increased risks as you proceed. Update your schedule dependencies as necessary, preserving a realistic activity network for all remaining project work. Before you finalize your revised documents, conduct an in-depth planning review, focusing on new risks and any consequences for work outside of your project.

Present your new project plans to your sponsor and stakeholders, and get their formal approval for any increases in project costs or modifications to delivered scope. For large changes, establish a revised baseline and work to manage stakeholder expectations for your modified project.

81. How can I effectively manage several small projects that don't seem to justify formal project management procedures?

General principles for running small projects are found in Problem 8. This problem focuses on using plans to track and control several simultaneous projects.

Initiating and Planning Small Projects

Small projects in most organizations tend not to vary a great deal from one to the next, so there are a number of things you can do to simplify the process of getting them going. Small projects may not require a great deal of formal process or overhead, but retaining control does require that you develop at least a minimum set of basic project documents. You may not need much, but it's always best to scale your project management processes to the work at hand.

Projects are often short because their deliverables are relatively simple. The deliverables are also frequently variations on a theme, so you can usually collect and document the requirements easily using forms or check-off sheets. This significantly reduces overhead and the possibility of missing something. Similarly, planning documents may be based on templates that describe the work normally performed in sufficient detail that you can develop plans for each new project with just some minor additions, deletions, and edits. If you lack these types of templates, begin developing them for your current projects, and save them to facilitate planning for future projects.

Set up a repository for project documents for each of your projects. Involve the contributors who will work with you in "fast-track" planning activities to capture what the project must do. Review the plans to ensure that all needed activities are listed, and at a minimum review their sequence and the overall project workflow. Doing this with yellow sticky notes on a wall or whiteboard may be sufficient to establish a logical work progression that will avoid problems and rework. Also do at least rough estimating for the required work, enough to verify that the overall project timing is believable.

Whether you are working with the people on your projects full-time or not, assign explicit owners for each project activity. Obtain a reliable commitment from each person to complete the work on time.

Projects that are small may not take all of your time, but they need what they need. Unless your projects have almost no staff or they involve a lot of "waiting" time where there is nothing that you need to manage, you will probably not be able to keep up with more than about six projects. If they are more complex, your limit will be smaller. If you take on more projects than you can reasonably keep up with, you will lose control.

Controlling Small Projects

Status collection and reporting also need not be an overwhelming production. If you are managing a set of projects that are all staffed using the same pool of people, you may be able to collect status on all of them together. Each week, request status on all open and due work from each of your contributors, and keep your (and their) overhead as low as you are able to by making the process for responding as simple as possible.

Whether or not the same people are working on all of your projects, you can reduce your status communication efforts by producing a single weekly report covering all of your projects. Keep your reporting simple, but include a clear, ongoing summary that shows your progress on each independent project.

One key for controlling multiple small projects is to not let them meander. Work to minimize changes and scope creep, and endeavor to avoid surprises at the end of the project. If you do a good job in specifying the deliverables at the start and not much changes in the course of a brief project, your closure should be straightforward.

82. What are good practices for managing complex, multi-site projects?

To control big complex projects or programs you need to manage a large team of contributors, complicated technology, and a hierarchy of interdependent schedules. Avoiding the pitfalls inherent in this requires technique and discipline (and luck).

Leading a Large Distributed Team

Guidance for setting up a large program is explored in Problem 21. Getting a large team of people headed in the same direction starts with very strong sponsorship from someone who has the respect of the people involved and who will fund and support an effective program start-up. You also will benefit from a vivid and compelling vision for the program that will motivate and inspire all who are involved.

Keeping people engaged requires a lot of communication, with at least monthly all-program meetings to discuss what is going on, and weekly meetings in between the program meetings for each of the project teams. An inviting and meaningful "open-door" policy—where anyone may ask anyone else about anything related to the program—also serves to increase involvement, whether people actually take advantage of it or not.

The program leader and any program staff also need to establish relationships and trust among all the project leaders, and encourage effective interactions throughout the program team.

To avoid some common pitfalls, periodically bring people together for scheduled face-to-face meetings to maintain motivation and teamwork on long programs, hold program-level monthly meetings at different times of the day so at least one will be when your remote contributors are awake and alert, and use all the means of communication available to you to maintain common understanding and effective coordination of your program team.

Dealing with Complex Technology

Managing complex technology is also a challenge on large programs. It begins with engaging skilled subject matter expertise and dealing with feasibility issues as early as possible. In order to effectively delegate work to independent teams that will be responsible for their execution, you must strive for coherent decomposition of the scope. You also will need to schedule periodic technical reviews during the program to detect problems and make adjustments.

The biggest technology-related pitfalls for programs usually relate to inadequate feasibility analysis and unexpected consequences of approved changes. Clearly define all program deliverables, particularly those where the work is outsourced. Large programs require very strong and formal specification change management to remain in control of complex technology. Be scrupulous in analyzing all proposed changes, and remain vigilant for unintended results following any you accept. Manage program-level issues promptly, especially when they relate to technical problems.

Managing a Hierarchy of Schedules

Programs depend on consistent schedules for all the included projects and an integrated timeline for the program as a whole. The process for identifying project interfaces and building integrated program schedules is outlined in Problem 56. To remain in control, periodically verify that all cross-project dependency agreements remain valid, especially after any personnel shifts or accepted specification changes. Also conduct risk reviews about once per month to pick up on emerging issues, and schedule overall program planning reviews at least twice per year to revalidate the objectives and to focus on detailed planning for the next phases of program work.

Establish a coherent, centralized program management information system that is organized to facilitate the needs of all the contributors and affords access to all pertinent program documentation.

Primary problems related to scheduling for large multi-site programs include significant work that falls through the cracks and is not included in any of the planned projects, failure to coordinate work around international holiday schedules, and inadequate cross-project coordination within the program.

Getting Lucky

Apart from sharing the observation that "luck is what happens when preparation meets opportunity," I can't help you much here.

83. How do I best deal with time zone issues?

In a perfect world, project teams would all sit together. This ensures ongoing robust informal communications and effective teamwork, and (mostly) lets everyone get adequate sleep. Real projects can't always co-locate, so you need to do what you can to compensate.

Planning for Around-the-Clock Staffing

There are some advantages to a distributed team. "Follow the sun" operations afford better coverage and might, for some types of activities, significantly reduce duration estimates. If the work is sufficiently simple that it can be quickly picked up and advanced by contributors working independently, assign it to one contributor in India for one half of the day and to another in the United States for the other half. Not all tasks can be decomposed at this level, but for those where it is possible you may be able to complete the work in about half the time.

Setting up meetings to support your team will inevitably be somewhat inconvenient. You may need to hold several meetings, including some that you may either need to delegate leadership for or plan to lose some sleep over. Leading a small global team a few years ago I had a few contributors in Shanghai, a subject matter expert in the UK, and I was in California. Our weekly team meetings were at 3 P.M. in China, 7 A.M. in England, and 11 P.M. for me. This was usually workable, except for the times when I had 6 A.M. teleconferences the following day. Work to minimize the pain of cross-time-zone meetings by moving them around occasionally and keeping alert for opportunities to take advantage of travel to catch people in more convenient locations.

Also be aware of the international dateline. The effective overlap across the Pacific is essentially only four days per week; Monday in Asia is still the weekend for North and South America, and the weekend starts in Asia before people in the Americas get to work on Friday.

Communicating Globally

Distributed teams depend heavily on asynchronous communications, especially e-mail. Take full advantage of electronic messaging of all types to support your project, but always follow up complicated information that you distribute with at least a telephone call to verify that it was received and understood. Never leave for the day with pending questions in your e-mail. If you wait to reply until the next morning, you will cost your remote contributors an extra whole day. Also, design your online project management information system to ensure that everyone can "self-serve" and retrieve the information he or she needs without waiting a day for you to show up at work.

Set up one-on-one meetings by telephone with each of your team members, finding a time during their workday when you are also at least somewhat alert. Project leaders on global projects need to be flexible, getting up early and staying up late to keep up with their projects. After any complicated telephone discussions or meetings, follow up in writing to summarize what was said or decided.

84. How can I manage changes to the project objective in the middle of my project?

Scope creep is one of the biggest problems on modern projects. There's an old saying: "Projects quickly get to 90 percent complete and stay there forever." This is not about incompetence or laziness; it's about projects where the rate of change exceeds the rate of progress. Managing this adequately requires setting up an effective change management process and then enforcing its use.

Setting the Foundation for Change Control

Project change control depends on a thoroughly defined scope that is supported by a credible baseline plan. Even a robust-looking plan will not help much if your project scope is poorly defined. Setting requirements is discussed in Problem 22, and establishing clear project priorities and a realistic project baseline (including a clearly defined scope) is covered in Problem 78. Effective change control requires a frozen scope against which proposed changes would be applied, and it relies on project priorities to ensure that any changes accepted are consistent with what is most important to your project.

To protect your baseline and defined scope, you will need a well-defined, sufficiently formal process to manage all specification changes. Unless your organization has an effective global process for doing this, plan to define (or refine) your own. Work with your team and stakeholders during initiation or planning to set the foundation for this, stressing the importance of a stable scope and the potential pain and damage to the project caused by poorly managed, chaotic change. Also obtain buy-in for your change process from your sponsor and management. Stress that the control afforded by a good process for managing changes will be instrumental in ensuring that you can deliver on the results they have requested. Controlling changes from managers and powerful stakeholders can be among the most damaging and difficult to manage. Dealing with these particular cases is explored more deeply in Problems 85 and 86, respectively.

Establishing an Effective Change-Control Process

All effective change-control processes are based on answering two questions: "What's it cost?" and "What's it worth?" Your process should provide a mechanism for anyone involved with the project to propose a change, but regardless of the source, always ask the submitter to include some initial cost-benefit analysis.

In defining the change management process, make the default disposition of all proposed changes "reject." Put the burden of proof that a change is necessary on the requester, and always ensure that any changes that you do accept are based on a good business case.

Consider the source for each change. Be skeptical of changes from within your team unless they directly relate to a current problem or issue you must resolve. Some of the worst examples of scope creep arise within project teams. (We are endlessly clever, and continually coming up with new, bright ideas.) If the source of the change is outside of your team, also be careful. Even for changes where the consequences (such as additional costs or time slippage) will be borne by a customer, modifying your project in flight can be a very poor idea.

Some change proposals will come in from your sponsor or management. Having a strong process that all of your stakeholders have accepted in advance is particularly important in these cases. If you do not have an approved, objective process in place prior to the change request from the people you work for, you will have a tough time saying "no" (and you may be unable to anyway, even with a good process in place).

Build a step requiring thorough, objective analysis into your change-control process. Work to verify any benefits claims made for each change, especially for changes that are not mandatory. Also verify what the change will do to your project's costs and timing through a review of your current plans. Consider potential unintended consequences, particularly for proposed changes on large, complex programs.

Set objective criteria for evaluating each change, rejecting all changes where the business case is poor (or based on questionable information), the change is materially in conflict with stated project priorities, or there could be unacceptable adverse consequences. Set the bar for acceptance particularly high for any changes that will materially affect your project baseline.

In addition to the default "reject" disposition, include possible responses for "accepted with modifications" and "not yet," as alternatives to "accepted." Use the other responses to deal with good ideas that may be only partially justified or would be more appropriate in a follow-on project. In addition to setting up decision criteria, establish roles for named individuals in the change process, including at least one person with the power to say "no" and make it stick. (This is often the project sponsor.)

Using Your Change-Control Process

When changes are submitted, capture key data for them in a tracking log and verify the submission form is complete. Return incomplete submissions to the person who sent it (or help him or her to finish it). Analyze each change promptly and meet to consider all queued changes on a regular schedule. Use your meeting to make a decision on each pending change, post the disposition on your change log in your project management information system, and provide feedback on your decisions directly to the individuals who submitted the changes.

For all accepted or partially accepted changes, review your planning and other project documents. Make updates as needed and communicate them to your team members and stakeholders. If an accepted change materially affects your baseline, review the changes with your sponsor and key stakeholders and gain their approval to revise your objectives.

85. How should I respond to increased demands from management after the project baseline has been set?

Managing changes submitted by sponsors and upper-level managers is a special case of scope change management. In general, your best defenses are a well-defined, objective process (as described in Problem 84) and clear presentation of any adverse consequences to the project. For changes you must absorb, work to minimize their impact.

Using Your Change Process

Establish and get support for a well-defined process from your sponsor as part of your initial project discussions. Use recent past problems and the pain and chaos of past projects where changes were not controlled well to justify an objective process with unambiguous decision criteria. Such a process is relatively easy to sell at project start-up, when the focus is on planning and logical analysis. Such a process can be very difficult to shoehorn into a project later, as the pressures of execution build and after proposed changes begin to surface.

Armed with an objective process that enables you to examine the realistic costs and benefits of each submitted change, you will have a strong defense against arbitrary changes. Insist that all changes be analyzed, regardless of their source. Be skeptical of projected benefits of changes, particularly where the change appears to be discretionary or optional. Be diplomatic but firm in documenting a thorough justification for each change, even those that originate with your management.

Also be scrupulous in analyzing consequences, including any impact to project timing, budget, or scope, especially where the change could have an effect on one of your project's top priorities. Also analyze other potential consequences of each change, such as additional overtime, loss of team motivation, or potential unintended effects.

Making Good Change Decisions

If the change appears to be mandatory, or it has a credible and compelling business justification, prepare to accept it. As with any accepted change, update your project documents and communicate the revisions. If the change is major, work with your sponsor in resetting your project baseline.

If the change is less than compelling, use your analysis to avoid accepting it. Vividly describe the consequences of the change, emphasizing any that directly conflict with stated project objectives. Because you are dealing with your management, you'll need to tread softly. One possible approach is to start with, "Yes, we can implement that change, but that will require these additional changes. . . ." Especially for changes proposed late in the project, describe what will have to be taken out of the project to compensate for what management proposes to add. Make the impact of the change clear, and recommend that it be rejected.

If your most logical arguments are ineffective, propose deferring the change request to be part of a later project or implementing it as a follow-on effort after you have completed your currently defined project. If all else fails, counterpropose that only some parts of the proposed change be accepted, trimming off the most harmful aspects of the change while retaining some of its benefits.

You are always at a disadvantage when debating with people higher up in the organization than you are, and sometimes they will force changes into your project despite your best and most logical arguments to avoid them. When this happens, document the recommendation you made and the reasons for it. Include honest analysis of the impact of the change in your status reporting, and revisit the change decision as part of your post-project retrospective analysis. Use your lessons-learned analysis of questionable management-commanded changes to tighten up your change process and to help you in handling similar situations on future projects.

86. How can I avoid issues with new stakeholders, especially on global projects?

Not all stakeholders are involved at the start of every project, especially on projects with long durations. As new players come into the mix for your work, make them aware of what you are doing and why, and work to understand their needs and interests. Endeavor to harmonize their requirements with your project, by using your change process and by involving them in ongoing project communications.

Identifying Stakeholders

Be proactive in your stakeholder analysis. Consider all those who are, should be, or even might be affected by or have an effect on your project. The more complete you can make your early stakeholder involvement, the better off you will be in the long run. If you are working on a local pilot of something that might be later rolled out worldwide, reach out to potential stakeholders and involve them in critiquing your scope. If you are developing a product that will be sold initially in only one market but you suspect would have appeal elsewhere, familiarize yourself with regulatory requirements and discuss possible needs in other locales. It is much easier to develop a deliverable with enough flexibility to conform to a range of initially documented standards than it is to retroactively force-fit a narrowly defined deliverable to meet unanticipated requirements.

Inevitably you will miss someone, and there will also be stakeholders who will become involved with your project as it is running for reasons you cannot control or anticipate. In these cases, you will need to establish good working relationships with your new stakeholders as they come into view.

Engaging New Stakeholders

When you identify new stakeholders, promptly set up a meeting to introduce yourself. Work to establish trust with your new stakeholders and place them in contact, if they are not already, with your other stakeholders and your sponsor. At least initially, assume that all new stakeholders are allies for your project; be open and friendly. Provide documents describing your project and offer access to the portions of your project management information system that are available to other stakeholders. Review the objectives and expectations you are pursuing, and explain the overall value of your project and its vision. Describe your progress to date, and lay out your plans for the remainder of the project.

Respond to any questions about your project candidly. Ask about any specific requirements or needs that your new stakeholder has. Show how your project addresses any that are presently part of your scope. Explicitly list any stated requirements that are not included in your project as it is presently defined. A process for effectively collecting customer and stakeholder requirements is explored in Problem 22.

Managing Project Changes

Explain your change management process (similar to that described in Problem 84) to your new stakeholders, and work to secure their buy-in for its use. For each listed requirement that is not already part of your project, document a change proposal and begin analyzing each one. As a sign of goodwill, plan to accept most small changes that don't conflict with your current scope if you can accommodate them without significant additional cost or other project impact. For changes that will represent noticeable changes to your project, use your change process to determine how to proceed. If the cost of a change will exceed its projected value, plan to reject the change. If the change as stated is inconsistent with the wishes of your existing stakeholders, engage all the individuals involved in discussions to resolve any conflicts before making any decisions. Engage them in negotiations where needed to revise the requested change as needed to balance the needs of all of your stakeholders. For changes that you intend to reject or defer, you may need to involve your sponsor in delivering the decision and to help you in managing stakeholder expectations.

If a requested change has significant benefits compared with its costs, use your change process to verify that accepting it is reasonable and appropriate. Determine the overall impact of the change before accepting it, and always consider possibilities for accepting it with modifications or committing to delivery of the specific requirements at a later time. If justified by a credible business case, plan to accept the change and modify your project scope. Before saying "yes," adjust your plans accordingly, and if the change will require any major shifts to your overall objective, work with your sponsor to reset your project baseline.

Communicate the disposition of all proposed changes to your stakeholders, whether accepted or not. Work to adjust stakeholder expectations to align them with your project's goals, involving your sponsor where necessary.

87. What should I do when team members fail to complete tasks, citing "regular work" priorities?

Ensuring follow-through begins with getting a credible commitment from the contributor who owns the work. Some techniques for this are discussed in Problem 48. Successful closure relies on proactive tracking and holding people to their commitments, as discussed in Problem 66. However, priorities do shift, so there are times when this may not be enough. Faced with delayed work that must be done, you need to first verify priorities, and verify the root causes. (The actual reasons for delayed delivery may not always be what people tell you.) If you are unable to restore reliable commitments for your project, you'll need to find alternatives and make project adjustments.

Verifying Work Priorities and Causes

If assigned project tasks are not being completed as planned, you need to find out why. Even when people tell you that they have conflicting higher priorities, that may not be the whole story. The list of possibilities for why people fail to do what they are supposed to do is quite lengthy, including:

▲ They have too much work overall.
▲ They need training or help to do the work.
▲ Their responsibilities and commitments are unclear.
▲ The work requires more authority than they have (or than they believe they have).
▲ They get no feedback on their work or they are punished for doing things correctly.
▲ They are rewarded for doing the wrong things.
▲ They don't have adequate documentation or job aids for their work.
▲ Their work environment makes doing their work difficult or impossible.

Meet one-on-one with your contributor and discuss his tasks to learn what is really going on. If he lacks training or the actual problems are unrelated to a conflict with other priorities, do what you can to resolve the issues. If there are higher priorities, determine what level of commitment is realistic for your team member. If your issue is with a part-time contributor, consult the advice in Problem 42. As you verify the amount of time available to your project, update your project resource analysis using the techniques discussed in Problem 60.

If your project's overall resource capacity appears diminished, set up meetings with the managers involved to discuss the situation. Review the priorities of your project's tasks relative to the other work with them. If your assigned contributor's other activities are both more important and urgent for the organization, you will probably need to adjust your project.

If, however, you discover that the actual priorities for your work are higher, use this information to reestablish the commitments and free up the effort needed to get your project activities completed. Escalate these discussions if necessary, and involve your sponsor and managers where appropriate to ensure that the work being done aligns with the organization's priorities. Work with the other managers and project leaders involved to modify the timing for their work as required.

If other priorities have eclipsed yours, though, you will need to find other options.

Adjusting Your Plans

One option to explore is getting help. The contributors whom you were counting on who are now unavailable may free up some of your funding. If so, explore options for locating substitute staff in your organization or contracting for outside help. If you have lost access to a contributor possessing critical skills, you may be able to fill the gap by training one of your other team members, or by recruiting the individual you were counting on to mentor someone on your staff through the work. In some cases, you may be able to find a way forward by revising a "make vs. buy" decision and purchasing a component instead of developing one that requires time and effort you no longer have.

Even if you do come up with an alternate path forward for your project, you may still need to make significant project changes. Revise estimates affected by the changes and develop a credible revised schedule for your project. Review your plans and update them to reflect all the necessary modifications. Most of the options you consider will probably have adverse cost implications, so discuss your plans with your sponsor and get approval in advance for any significant budget increases. Work with your sponsor to reset the baseline for your project if necessary, and communicate all significant changes to your stakeholders.

88. What is the best way to manage my project through reorganizations, market shifts, or other external changes?

External changes that affect projects are common. Protecting (and even improving) your project management processes during organizational changes is explored in Problem 20. This problem focuses on preserving your project objectives through proactive monitoring and by effectively dealing with changes.

Anticipating Changes

Change occurs frequently in some project environments, and it can substantially disrupt your work. You can significantly minimize the impact on your work if you see it coming and prepare for imminent changes in advance.

One powerful technique to help you see changes on the horizon is risk identification. You can uncover a wide variety of potential threats by periodically brainstorming risks or asking people to tell you about external factors that might hurt your project. Assess the risks you uncover, focusing particularly on risks that could have a major impact.

Informal communications with your team and stakeholders can be another fertile source of information on potential external changes. Ask about rumors and probe for things that people are worried or concerned about. As you discuss scenarios, review the specific consequences that a possible change might represent for your project.

Another early indication of priority changes and other shifts that could affect your project is when the work done by people from other organizations begins to slip, as discussed in Problem 87.

When conducting project reviews, as described in Problem 94, take advantage of your risk management evaluation. Consider how you could respond to future changes that people are concerned about.

If a rumored or probable change appears imminent, gather your team and discuss responses as soon as you discover it. Determine how you can detect that a change is coming and assign someone on your team to monitor the situation. Seek a trigger event that signals changes you are concerned about that gives you as much advanced warning as possible.

Managing Through Change

If something external to your project changes, take action. If you have relevant contingency plans, begin using them. If organizational priorities are changing, protect your relative priority as best you can using the value of your project; the influence of your sponsor and stakeholders; and, if you are near completion, the fact that you are almost done. If the change results in your losing your project sponsor, take advantage of the advice in Problem 17. In general, position your project as well as possible to minimize the change's impact.

External changes may result in specific modifications to your project that you will need to manage. If there are necessary scoping changes, use your change management process to evaluate and implement what is required, as outlined in Problem 84. When major changes occur outside your project, consider scheduling a project review to update your plans and reconfirm your objectives, as discussed in Problem 94.

Even if there appear to be no huge changes to your project objectives, it's good practice to review your project baseline with your sponsor and spend some time confirming expectations with your stakeholders following a big external shift. Following significant organizational change, your sponsor and key stakeholders may not remain in a position to continue their commitment to your project. Some external events, such as a major competitor's announcement of a product that eclipses yours, could even result in project cancelation.

89. How should I deal with having too many decision makers?

Although it is not entirely desirable to have a very large number of people involved with decisions, the fact is some decisions will have a lot of stakeholders. To make decisions work you will need sufficient consensus (or at least acceptance), so you must involve at least the principal people from whom you need buy-in.

Involving the Right People

For some decisions there will be one autocratic decision maker. For others you may seek unanimity from a team of collaborators. For most decisions, though, you will deal with some variation in between these two extremes. Although having a single person dictate all decisions is fast, and in emergencies may be necessary, for project decision making this usually doesn't work very well. Unless team members, stakeholders, and others who may be affected by decisions are involved with the decisions, they may not accept them. When too many "command and control" decisions are inflicted on a team, the members will become demotivated and may eventually quit. That said, decision processes requiring that everyone agree don't work very well either. They are excessively time-consuming and may never come to closure.

For a given decision, list each person who could be involved. Determine who is ultimately accountable for the decision. It could be you as the project leader, your sponsor, or some other person. Use a "RACI" matrix to categorize everyone who is involved. Assign the people who must participate in making the decision as "Responsible," including all who must cooperate or could block implementation of the decision. Assign one and only one owner to be "Accountable" for the decision, ideally yourself. Assign people who could impact the effectiveness of the decision as "Consulted," and assign those who need to know about it as "Informed."

Discuss the decision to be made with all the "R" people, and confirm that each will participate in the process. Also consider directly involving any of the "C" or "I" people, but include them only if you can come up with a compelling reason or if an "R" person strongly recommends it.

Understanding Issues and Options

Meet with the people who are to participate and agree on a clear statement of the decision at hand. Also clearly define and document any constraints you are facing, and confirm the decision process you plan to use.

For binary decisions such as those requiring only a "yes" or "no," a discussion followed by a simple vote may settle the question. For more complex decisions where there may be many possible outcomes (for example, determining what to include in project scope when working with a diverse group of stakeholders), you'll benefit from a more structured process. If some or all of the people involved are geographically separated, refer to some of the ideas in Problem 90.

Brainstorm suggested criteria that should be considered in making the decision without debate or criticism. Develop a single list including all of them and prioritize the list through discussion or by using a technique such as "multivoting" (where each person gets a certain number of votes to apply however he or she pleases). If any of the listed criteria lack support and there is agreement to drop them, cross them off. Throughout the decision process, encourage all to participate equally. Monitor for excessive input from strong personalities and by people participating who have more position power or authority, and draw out participants who are too quiet.

Next, focus on decision options as a team. Again without debate or criticism, let people list their preferred recommendations. When you have collected the options, discuss any of them that are unclear and consolidate any that appear redundant. Consider how well each alternative meets your defined decision criteria, and through discussion or weighted averaging using a spreadsheet or similar tool, determine which option best meets your criteria.

Making a Decision

Consider the top option, allowing people to raise any significant objections. Discuss any pitfalls, possible unintended consequences, and risks. If you find strong reasons to not accept the option that appears to best meet your stated decision criteria, loop back and review the original criteria. Adjust your criteria as appropriate, and continue your discussions and systematic analysis to strive for closure.

Discuss any objections that arise and work to address them. If the decision preferred by most remains strongly objected to by some, explore whether making adjustments to it might help. Avoid having one person or a small group dominate your final decision process, and make the final selection process as objective as possible. Strive to reach a consensus decision that all will accept.

If you come to an impasse where a few key people remain opposed to the decision, use your influence to attempt to secure at least acceptance of the recommendation favored by the majority so that you may proceed. As a last resort, escalate the decision to your sponsor or upper management in your organization, providing them with the results of your analysis and your majority recommendation. Once a decision has been made, communicate it to all people involved, update any affected project documents, and put it into effect.

90. How should I manage multi-site decision making?

Involving members of a distributed team in decision making begins with using a well-defined objective process such as that described in Problem 89. It also involves investing the time required to ensure that all who need to be involved take part, regardless of their location, and will accept the decision.

Engaging Stakeholders

For decisions that will affect people who are geographically separated, it can be difficult to identify the people who need to be involved. Once identified, it can also be hard to get them to participate in making the decision. For example, decisions affecting a lot of people across a large program with many distributed project teams can be quite complicated, and they may appear to be more of a distracting time waster than an urgent imperative. If you are responsible for such decisions, a lot of the responsibility for locating and gaining the cooperation of the right people will fall on your shoulders.

Begin determining who needs to be involved by discussing the issues requiring a decision with key stakeholders, such as project leaders, subject matter experts, key contributors, and program or project staff members. Through your discussions, identify the people who must buy in to the decision and approach each of them individually to gain his or her commitment to help make the decision.

In particular, find and engage the individual who has the largest stake in the process. Use your key stakeholder's reliance on making a good decision to enlist his or her help in organizing and running the process. Many of your meetings will probably be on the telephone. Set them up to be at a time convenient for the other person, and do your best to make them as effective as possible.

Framing the Decision

One effective way to approach distributed decision making is to take a step-by-step approach. Begin working with your key stakeholder to state the issue requiring a decision. Document it, and then discuss it with all the other participants in the process, one by one. Edit as you go, using the feedback you pick up. Work to craft a coherent problem statement that reflects the concerns and issues important to all involved, and end by returning to your principal stakeholder. Using a "one-sheet" technique allows each person to contribute but ensures that the final version will fairly reflect everyone's perspective. As described in Problem 23, this "one version of the truth" process can be very effective for generating consensus with a diverse, distributed team. While you are collecting and integrating feedback, discourage people from jumping directly to problem solving and final decision proposals; focus initially on getting the question framed correctly. After you have met with everyone, verify that all your participants agree that the question is appropriate and that it makes sense.

Proceed with your process, collecting suggestions for decision criteria, and then follow up by collecting potential decision options from everyone. Based on the inputs you collect, craft a potential decision recommendation with your key stakeholder. Discuss the proposal with all the others, one by one, marking it up with suggestions as you proceed. After you have discussed the proposal with everyone, share the resulting markup with all.

Committing to a Decision

If there is general agreement, publish the decision and put it into effect. If residual issues and objections remain, discuss options for minimizing them. To help generate consensus, keep the consequences of failing to come to agreement visible. Consider bringing people face-to-face to work out particularly serious disagreements. As a last resort, escalate completely intractable decisions to your upper management for resolution.

Communicate the decision to all affected, and update any documents in your project management information system so that everyone will have the information necessary to move ahead.

91. What can I do when people claim that they are too busy to provide status updates?

Getting cooperation from your team members for project management processes in general is covered in Problem 36. Encourage effective status cooperation using carrots and sticks. If that doesn't work, look for alternative methods to keep up with what is going on.

Providing Encouragement: Carrots

One of the most critical factors for status collection is keeping the process as simple as possible. If you expect a lot of detail or make people figure out exactly what status they need to provide, you will get only intermittent results. It's better to send each contributor a list of all his or her current and approaching activities with a space for a date and another space for an optional comment. (Past dates signify completion, and future dates show expected completion.) Make the reporting process easy and it will leave little room for excuses. Periodically, ask your team members to comment on your status process and request suggested improvements. If your process needs improvement, fix it.

For people who miss once in a while, especially if they are not local, send a reminder or call them on the telephone. Be persistent and willing to ask more than once.

If you have team members who are chronically unreliable in providing input, meet with them to talk about the situation. If possible, meet face-to-face for your discussion. Explain how you use the status and why it's important. If there are barriers or problems to their reporting process, discuss and work to resolve them. If there are issues with how the information is used, such as criticism or punishment following submission of bad news, figure out how to avoid it (as well as any other motivation for "gaming" the information, as discussed in Problem 68).

If the issue truly is that your contributor has more assigned work to do than he or she can handle, review the assignments that everyone is carrying and rebalance project work more equitably. Overall, encourage cooperation with your status collection process by thanking people for sending it (even the bad news), and visibly use the status you collect to report on and run your project.

Dealing with Slackers: Sticks

It is always better to get results through praise than through punishment, but that may not always work. If some of your team members are completely uncooperative despite your best efforts, warn them that future project reports will begin to include a note highlighting their missing input. If the warning does not improve matters, add a "red stoplight" problem indicator to the list of current project issues, along with an objective description of the status collection problems you are having.

In extreme cases, you may also need to consider escalating the matter to the individual's manager (or to your manager, if your problem contributor reports to you). Escalation over something like this that seems minor may appear to be overkill, but a lack of cooperation with status reporting can be a leading indicator of more significant behavior or performance problems.

Seeking Alternatives

Another thing you may want to consider, particularly if your current process is not as effective or straightforward as you would like, is rethinking your status process. There are situations in projects where progress on principal activities is directly visible to you. If it is more expedient, pull the information together yourself and show it to your task owners for a quick review. Remember, it's your project and without adequate status you cannot do your job. Even if you end up adopting a process that is somewhat harder on you, it might be your best choice for staying on top of what is happening in your project.

There may be cases where getting help in collecting status will improve cooperation. If you have several people at a remote site, you might be able to enlist the help of someone there to assemble all of the information and send it to you. On large programs, there may be people on the program staff who are in good positions to easily assemble status for projects and functions. Consider any options for status collection that are effective and minimize the overall effort and overhead.

There may also be practical options for automating the status collection process. Consider Web-based tools or survey techniques to streamline your process. If people are already using online time tracking or other computer-based systems, investigate if there are options to use them to facilitate your project collection status.

92. How can I effectively manage projects where the staff is managed by others?

Getting project results when you lack authority over members of your team is a big challenge for most project leaders. It begins with establishing and maintaining good relationships and trust, as described in Problems 41 and 42. You can also use process, influence, and metrics to better stay in control of your project.

Building a Foundation of Trust

Good project management depends on effective teamwork, so strive to establish a friendly working relationship with each of your team members. To maintain trust throughout your project, practice integrity and credibility—mean what you say, and deliver on what you say you will do. Open and honest relationships provide the solid foundation that you will need to get through the bumpy parts of your project.

Influencing Others

Even if you do not directly manage some of your contributors, your influence on them can be substantial. Some of your influence results from your position as the project leader. You have some "position" power based on the fact that you were selected to lead the project by an influential sponsor. You may also have the support of powerful stakeholders and others who want the project to succeed. The vision and purpose of the project may also be an important factor for your team members, so keeping the reasons you are all undertaking the project visible will enhance your influence. Discussing the project with the managers of your contributors will assist you in enlisting their support, which can augment your leverage in dealing with your team. Finally, one very effective way to gain influence is to ask for it. As the project leader, look your individual staff members in the eye and request that they cooperate and commit to the project. If they agree, they will be providing you with some influence and authority over them. Your actual clout will probably still not be very substantial, but your apparent authority may be sufficient to keep your project moving (if you don't abuse it).

You also have the ability to offer and deliver things people appreciate in exchange for their cooperation. You may assume you have little to offer, but that's not so. As the project leader, you can provide desirable assignments, training opportunities, responsibility, praise, recognition, and much more. You can do favors for people, either in exchange for things you need now or against future situations where you will need to call them in. Giving and getting are fundamental to human interactions; effectively using the principles of reciprocity can provide you with significant influence and control over your project.

Establishing Processes

Documented processes are another technique that project leaders can use to control their work. Start each project with a discussion of methods to be used, focusing on those needed to avoid problems on past projects. Take advantage of recent memories to gain buy-in for project processes that will help you maintain control. Take full advantage of any useful processes that are recommended or mandated by your organization. Collect explicit buy-in from your team members to follow good project management processes, and use their agreement to guide the work on your project. You will find additional suggestions on process adoption in Problem 12.

Using Measurement

As your project progresses, one additional tool you have for control is the power of the pen. In your reporting, you will include metrics on project progress, such as objective data on progress and results. Measurement drives behavior, so you can use positive data to recognize and reward accomplishments. Negative information that you report (or threaten to report) can be a powerful aid in helping you control your project.

93. How can I minimize unsatisfactory deliverable and timing issues when outsourcing?

Satisfactory outsourcing of project work begins with a good selection and engagement process, as described in Problem 29. To keep things under control, you need to set and enforce contract terms and communicate effectively.

Establishing Contract Terms

Seek contractors and vendors who have experience and a history of accomplishments that will justify your confidence in their ability to execute. Check references and ask about prior work. Where possible, request work samples to evaluate their quality and suitability for your needs.

Once you have selected an outsourcing partner who you believe could meet your project's requirements, develop contract terms and conditions that will maximize the likelihood that your vendor will deliver what you need. Review the contract thoroughly for clarity on deliverables, dates, and key requirements. Clearly define the process to be used or any changes or contract amendments. Ensure that payment terms are unambiguous, and consider adding incentives and penalties aligned with your project's objectives. Tie all payments to tangible results delivered and explicit progress measures. To manage budget risk, avoid "time and materials" pricing in the contract.

Minimize the inclusion of any specialized or unique terms that will require extensive legal or management review and hold up contract approval. Once the terms are set, obtain all the necessary signatures and get to work promptly.

Communicating Effectively

Establish a good working relationship with any individuals who will work directly as part of your team and others in their organization with liaison responsibilities. Meet with the people you will work with face-to-face at least initially, and set up weekly one-on-one discussions with your principal contacts. Use both formal and informal communications to build trust and collegial relationships. Involve all of the contract workers on your project staff in your planning and other project meetings whenever possible; make them as much a part of your team as your organizational policies will permit.

Establish an effective routine for collecting status at least weekly. For status, don't settle for "Things are going well." Verify progress as you proceed using interim deliverables such as documentation, inspections, prototypes, pilots, mock-ups, models, and testing. Be scrupulous about monitoring that work is being completed as documented in the contract.

Use the contract terms for incremental payments to ensure that the work, especially work performed where you cannot observe it, remains on track. When payments are due or invoices are received, verify that the work is satisfactory. If it is, approve the payments promptly.

94. How should I manage reviews for lengthy projects?

For most projects, you can plan about six months into the future with reasonable confidence. Beyond this planning horizon, things can become somewhat murky, so longer projects require periodic planning reviews. These reviews are to revalidate the objectives and project plans and are also good opportunities to audit processes and reinforce teamwork.

Reviewing Plans

To keep plans and expectations current on long-duration projects, schedule a planning review about every three to six months. The best times for reviews are at project decision and transition points, such as fiscal boundaries, major milestones, the ends of life-cycle phases, and staffing changes. Involve all of your core project team in the review, as well as others who should contribute to your planning. Plan to hold project review meetings face-to-face whenever possible, especially if you have a distributed project team.

The duration of a plan review will vary, from a few hours for a project undertaken by a small colocated team to several days for a major program. Your agenda will be similar to that for a project start-up workshop, focusing on planning and shared understanding of the project. Begin with a review of the overall objectives and the project charter to reinforce what you are attempting to accomplish. Also focus on detailed planning for upcoming work, with particular emphasis on specific deliverables, activities, assignments, estimates, and dependencies. Discuss any changed assumptions or constraints, and determine how any changes will affect the project. Also, include a risk review during the meeting to identify and deal with new threats and potential problems.

Follow up the review by updating all affected project documents, and bring all the information in your project management information system up-to-date. If your review results in major project changes, present them to your sponsor. If necessary, get your sponsor's approval and reset your project baseline.

Checking Your Processes

Use your review to conduct a mini "lessons learned," and take a moment to think about your recently completed work. Identify good practices that worked so you can repeat them. Also examine any recent difficulties, and consider changes you need to make to avoid similar issues in your upcoming work. Problem 75 discusses implementing mid-project process changes.

Recharging Your Team's Batteries

Long projects can become boring and result in lowered motivation. A project review is a great time to remind people why the project is important and to recognize major accomplishments. Use the occasion to reconnect people to the project and to build and maintain the teamwork and trust you'll need in the next phase of the project. Use the meeting to explicitly thank your contributors for their past work. If possible, schedule some time for a team event during or immediately following the review.

95. What should I do to establish control when taking over a project where I was not involved in the scoping or planning?

Sometimes you must assume leadership for a project that someone else started. To do this well, you must keep things going while you maintain (or establish) team cohesion, review and update the plans, and get to know your stakeholders.

Keeping the Plane in the Air

When you are tossed into the middle of a running project, your first order of business will be to keep it going. Some projects needing a new leader are in good shape, because the former leader's departure had nothing to do with the state of the project. Other projects, however, may need serious attention to correct problems, and this can be true even for some projects that appear on the surface to be running smoothly. Whatever your initial impressions, you will need to rapidly assess what people are doing and, unless you detect serious issues, keep them doing it. If there are adequate documents and plans available, quickly use them to do a thorough cycle of status collection to identify any significant variances. If the planning information is thin or nonexistent, meet with each project team member to discuss what he or she is up to and plans to do next. Document what you learn and prepare a status report summarizing the state of the project.

Establishing Relationships and Teamwork

Schedule time with each assigned contributor to meet one-on-one and get to know each other. Discuss roles and responsibilities, and begin building trust. When you inherit a project with a team that's already in place, you'll want to do this fast. Accelerate the process by discussing any past associations or colleagues you have in common with your contributors, and use these connections to help you quickly establish relationships with your new team. Other ideas to help with this can be found in Problem 34.

Making the Plans Your Own

Regardless of how good the project plans and other documentation that you inherit appear to be, you will need to thoroughly review them, and update them as necessary to create plans that you understand and believe in. On one of my earliest projects, I was asked to step in as leader shortly after a project had begun. I foolishly accepted the planning information I was handed, and I began running the project. The project in fact had unrealistic deadlines and assumptions that were not credible. By the time I realized my error several weeks into the project, I was in the midst of an ugly mess, with people arguing and fighting, and having to work huge amounts of overtime to even come close to the stated goals. Had I initially verified what I was told, we would have avoided much of this grief. Although ultimately the project ended "successfully," by the end there was so much scorched earth and bad feeling that it taught me a lesson I will never forget.

To make the time you need to review (or create) plans, you may need to delegate some day-to-day leadership tasks temporarily to one of your contributors. As you work to come up to speed this may be for the best anyway, because a senior person on your new team may well know a lot more about the project than you do. Begin your review by assessing the project requirements. Meet with the project sponsor and discuss the requirements and the overall project objective. Ask your sponsor about project stakeholders and how they connect to the project. Note any obvious holes, "fuzziness," or conflicts that you detect in your review or during any of these discussions.

Next, start to inspect any existing plans. Using the status information you have collected and any existing plans, validate that all work marked completed is in fact done. Identify any issues and gaps in the planning, and verify ownership of all upcoming work. Involve all your project contributors in your reviews, and invite people to critique the plans and update them to reflect the work that actually remains. It may be helpful to organize a project review (as described in Problem 94) to assist you in verifying (or building) the plans.

In the process of reviewing your plans, also quickly review the overall project management processes in use. If they appear satisfactory, plan to live with them. If you detect any significant problems, note the issues and make it a priority to deal with them soon.

Adjusting Expectations

If you detect significant problems in your requirements analysis or plan review, meet with your sponsor to discuss them. If you find that significant changes are necessary, use your data to negotiate them and reset your project baseline to be realistic. Problem 78 covers principled negotiations and dealing with unrealistic project constraints.

Following your discussions with your sponsor, reach out to your stakeholders to gather their perspectives on the project. When you meet, present any changes that will be necessary. Discuss the objectives that you are pursuing and talk about their expectations for the project. Work to gain their confidence and support for you as the leader for the remainder of the project.

96. What should I consider when adopting technology-based communication tools?

Some of the purposes served by remote communications are explored in Problem 71, and Problem 72 focuses on how best to communicate globally. This problem outlines some communications tools for voice, computer networking, video, and electronic messaging, including some of their advantages and disadvantages.

Using Voice Communications

Audio teleconferencing is ubiquitous and inexpensive. Project teams make extensive use of it to meet with distant team members and others. It has many advantages: It requires no special equipment, it is easy to set up, most organizations have permanent infrastructure for it, and commercial services are also widely available and inexpensive. The principal disadvantages are that it's not as effective as face-to-face communications, and it can be very hard to keep people's attention for meetings lasting more than an hour or so. This is especially true for people who participate in meetings using regular telephone handsets where most of the discussion is in a room using a speakerphone.

There is also increasing use of mobile phones and "Web phone" software on projects these days. Both technologies increase the options for timing and locations available for telephone connections, and they may significantly lower costs. Unfortunately, these technologies also often represent significant reductions in audio quality and reliability. If you find this to be a problem, discourage their use for important calls and regular meetings.

Using Computer Networking

Another commonplace technology for remote meetings is Web-enabled sharing of computer displays. There are two primary types of technology for this: one supporting dynamic display sharing among a small

237

number of workstations, and another that requires setup in advance and is capable of showing a single display on a large number of other computers.

For a small project team or where people can gather in a limited number of locations, dynamic "network meeting place" software is an effective way to allow everyone to see what is on remote computer screens and permit a succession of people to "drive" the meeting. The cost of this sort of communication is very low, as it is often available as part of standard workstation infrastructure. Most of these applications can serve at least a half dozen workstations pretty well, but as the number grows the overhead and slow response starts to interfere with the effectiveness of this technique. It's useful for sharing documents, graphs, and other visual materials that are already computer based but can be inconvenient for other images, and it's ineffective for showing participants' faces.

For presentations that are mostly broadcast, one-way communications, the other type of "webinar" application software is more appropriate. Dozens or even hundreds of computers can simultaneously see what is being presented, but the shared screen needs to be set up in advance and is limited to one workstation, or at best a small number. This technology is very effective for periodic "all hands" program meetings, where most of the information used to inform a large community of remote contributors can be prepared in advance. There may be costs involved with setting up and running meetings with this software; if so, plan for the estimated expense in your budget. For the receiving participants, normally only a Web browser is required, but in some cases the computer used for presenting may need special hardware, or at least be running application-specific software. This style of Web-enabled sharing can also be set up to support at least low-resolution images of the presenters if the central workstation is equipped with cameras and appropriate switching capability.

Whichever type of Web-sharing software you are planning to use, test the connections in advance, especially for distant participants. If any of your contributors are not inside the network you plan to use, arrange for the access that they will need in advance to negotiate firewalls and other security barriers.

Using Video Communications

Videoconferencing is also becoming fairly commonplace. It provides the same "real-time" conversational support of audio conferences, but also some of the interaction of face-to-face meetings by showing images of the participants. When the video quality is high enough, the experience can approximate an in-person meeting, but most setups fall far short of this. Using the highest-quality video equipment and rooms for team meetings may be inconvenient to arrange and does consume time for travel and setup. Even in organizations where there is a well-established network of specialty video rooms, the project may bear significant direct expense to use it. If so, budget for the costs if you plan to take advantage of these facilities.

Video setups also add to your facilitation overhead. The need to point cameras, switch back and forth from presentation slides and other visual information, and monitor what is sent and received may add significant distractions to your meetings, especially if you need to do all of this and lead your meeting. If the pitfalls of videoconferencing appear to exceed its value, consider more convenient audio options combined with computer networking to realize many of the same results.

Workstation-based "videophone" applications are also becoming more popular for point-to-point communications. If you have the right hardware and sufficient network bandwidth to support it, this can be a useful way to add your smiling face to regularly scheduled one-on-one meetings with distant staff. The size and picture quality of the images may leave something to be desired, but video calls can nevertheless add a useful dimension to your individual interactions.

Using Electronic Messaging

Most important electronic messaging for projects remains in the domain of e-mail. E-mail is the foundation for most complex communication for distributed teams, because it provides an audit trail, it's reliable and easy to use, and it does not require that the sender and receiver of the messages both be active at the same time. It is an essential tool for following up on conversations, discussions in meetings, and other communications where things could easily be forgotten or overlooked. Written communication does have significant drawbacks, however. What you write can be easily misinterpreted, especially when it contains emotional content—or even seemingly emotional content. Studies of human communications conclude that the vast majority of meaning in a face-to-face exchange comes from the body language and emphasis used in speaking, with only a small portion being carried by the words. When sending an e-mail or other message, all you have are the words. Review all your e-mails (and other writing) carefully for clarity and completeness, and reconsider carefully any portions that could be misinterpreted or interpreted as criticism.

To maximize the utility of e-mail communications, establish standards to increase the visibility of important information and decrease clutter, particularly if you are leading a large team. Define code phrases or sets of symbols to be used in subject lines to identify time-sensitive communications, and establish ground rules for marking messages "urgent." Also set guidelines for using "reply to all" on broadcast messages (in general, never reply to all), and maintain centralized distribution lists for key functions to ensure that the most current list of recipients will be used when sending crucial information.

Today's technology also provides a blizzard of newer ways to connect one-on-one with others in real time, including mobile text messages and computer-based instant messaging. There are also endless variations these days on social networking. All of this can substantially increase your ability to connect with your team members who embrace these communications. Before diving too deeply into their use, though, investigate what your team members will accept and won't find annoying. Your goal is to build trust and improve relationships, not to drive people away. Establish guidelines and etiquette for any techniques you do decide to adopt. Avoid interrupting people too often with your communication, and be mindful of potential distraction when you know they are deep in thought. People take about twenty minutes to return to full mental "speed" following an interruption, so use messaging (and telephone calls) sparingly if you are expecting your contributors to get much work done. As with phone calls, plan to follow up anything you transmit that is complicated with an e-mail to provide a permanent record.

Also, before adopting any new messaging technology, review the boundaries set by your organization for acceptable communications technology. Always observe established guidelines for security, confidentiality, and protecting proprietary information.

97. How should I select and implement software tools for project documentation, scheduling, and planning?

The tools available to help project leaders do their job range from very low tech to expensive, complicated computer applications. Communications tools are discussed in Problem 96, and considerations for tools applicable to large, multi-team programs are covered in Problem 98. The focus here is on selecting tools for planning and for managing information on typical projects.

Choosing Scheduling Tools

For very small projects, even the lowest-capability computer-scheduling tools may be overkill. A combination of diagrams on easel pages, yellow sticky notes for your work breakdown structure and activity network modeling, and a suite of standard office software applications should be more than enough to understand, plan, and track a mini-project.

For midsized projects, though, with dozens of activities and several months' duration, computer tools become more appropriate. Computer tools fall into two categories: low-end software with modest capacities for single users, and higher-capability, server-based products for larger projects and programs supporting multiple users.

Low-end products have several significant advantages, including lower cost, minimal hardware requirements, a modest learning curve, plentiful training opportunities, lots of available examples and templates, and many other people who use the software and can serve as mentors. There are also disadvantages for lower-end tools. They have limited capacity, so they do not deal as well with large projects having hundreds of tasks. Because they are stand-alone applications running on a single computer, linking related projects is strictly manual and can be difficult to keep up-to-date. Also, while low-end tools do an adequate job supporting duration estimates, task dependencies, and critical path analysis, their capabilities for resource analysis and effort tracking are generally rudimentary and difficult to use.

For larger projects or programs with many cross-project dependencies, the higher cost and steeper learning curve for more capable tools may be justified. Such tools provide more robust resource modeling, and many have additional features such as Monte Carlo risk analysis. Because they are server based, though, there may be access and response time issues for global projects. Offline capabilities are also an issue for these products, even for display and reporting purposes.

The primary consideration for choosing a tool for most projects, though, is alignment with peers, associated projects, and organizational standards. You are always better off using a tool that fits with your environment than picking one that might be nominally superior but that puts you out of sync with the folks you need to work with.

Managing Information

For very small projects, a file server or even a rudimentary Web site might be sufficient for your information storage needs. (For old-school project leaders managing a co-located team, a project file or notebook may even be enough.)

For typical projects, though, collaboration tools for file sharing and network storage are commonplace. Your principal objectives are to establish a well-organized project management information (PMIS) system and to ensure your team members have good access to it. Problem 33 describes the main considerations in setting up a PMIS. In most situations, the capabilities available to you will be chosen at the organization level, though you may have some choices available. At a minimum, you'll need functionality that provides file storage in a hierarchy of folders. You will also want to have the ability to fine-tune access and security settings so not everyone on the project has the same ability to update files. It's best to restrict the ability to delete files to a very small number of people, perhaps only yourself. Automatic version maintenance is useful to ensure that you have a good history base for your lessons-learned analysis and for later reference. Other desirable features include network-based list and calendar functions, e-mail alerts to inform you of updates, and the ability to post news items on a main access portal page.

If your organization has high-capability knowledge management software available, consider using it for your project PMIS. You will find more on high-end knowledge management systems in Problem 98.

98. What should I consider when setting up software tools I will be using to coordinate many interrelated projects?

Depends on:
- ▲ Regulations and industry standards
- ▲ Organizational requirements
- ▲ Program management office (PMO) recommendations

Managing Program Information

Large programs are typically subject to a lot of rules and guidelines. Assess all the information requirements that your program will need to comply with, and determine how you plan to meet them. If there are significant long-term requirements for providing permanent storage of project data related to health, safety, environmental, or other legal obligations, plan to establish (or take advantage of existing) infrastructure to conform. Estimate any necessary costs and include them in your resource plans and project budget. If your program is expected to observe any organizational or PMO requirements, determine how best to deal with them, too.

Large programs generate a great deal of information. Setting up an effective project or program management information system (or PMIS, as described in Problem 33) is essential for control and coordination of ongoing work. Organize your online data so that your distributed project team members can easily find what they need.

If the information infrastructure available to you appears inadequate or you will be establishing a knowledge management hierarchy from scratch, investigate options that will provide advanced capabilities to increase utility and ease of use. Consider software products that provide for multiuser check-out/check-in, coordinated updating, automated version maintenance, alias naming capability that allows information in a single file to be accessed from several places in the hierarchy, "key word in context" searching, tailored security, and other advanced access functions. More basic offerings can provide hierarchical network folder structures and some access security and control, but such modest capabilities can present problems for large, complex programs.

Document your program's staffing hierarchy clearly using a well-organized roster containing an up-to-date list of all the contributors involved in your program. Include roles, responsibilities, project affiliations, and full contact information for everyone, especially for the project leaders, program staff, and subject matter experts.

Delegate responsibility to an owner at the program level for managing the information in your PMIS and for supporting all of your users. Ensure that your program team has sufficient expertise in all the technical tools you are using, and will be able to provide adequate support to all program contributors. Work with the vendors of your software tools to keep your versions current. Coordinate any upgrades or changes required so they will not disrupt your program.

Coordinating Program Plans and Monitoring Progress

Work to establish access and use of common computer scheduling tools for all the projects within the program. Provide planning templates and involve program staff in project startup workshops and planning meetings to ensure overall consistency.

Adopt computer-based project management software that can support the size and other requirements of your program, and ensure that it is sufficiently compatible with the corresponding tools used by all of the project leaders. Using centralized, high-end tools for this can have a number of advantages, as outlined in Problem 97. If you choose to adopt a sophisticated project management tool, provide adequate training for all users and establish adequate expertise on your program team to keep things running smoothly, and provide advice and mentoring to others. Realistically assess the costs and effort required, and budget accordingly. In addition to the costs, consider the processes, both automated and manual, that you will need to establish and maintain to synchronize your hierarchy of plans and schedules. Server-based, centralized program tools can also support online time tracking and resource monitoring. If you plan to take advantage of this, estimate the time required to set up the database and include it in your plans.

Also standardize your processes for status collection and reporting throughout your program. Use compatible formats for data collection, and coordinate project-level reporting with program reporting to ensure consistency. If you plan to assemble status data online by collecting inputs using a high-end project management software tool, set up the information on activities, projects, resource categories, and other data in the database. To facilitate its use, provide adequate access and training for all program contributors.

99. How should I realistically assess the success and value of my project management processes?

Measuring project success can be a surprisingly difficult and confusing topic. Because by definition projects are all different, direct comparisons are perilous. Also, it's never easy to reach agreement on exactly what project "success" is. The most common interpretations of project success relate to the ultimate value of the deliverable. What your project results are worth depends on quite a few factors, most of which are completely out of your control and have little to do with project management. That said, there are useful ways to evaluate your project processes, and delivering value is both more likely and a lot more efficient when you manage your projects well.

Measuring Variance

At the end of a project, there are many actual numbers to compare with the estimates and other forecasts you made earlier. Comparing achieved performance with predictions provides useful feedback for fine-tuning your processes and improving the precision and accuracy of future project plans. Comparing duration and cost estimates with actual performance will show you where your estimating processes are working and where they are wildly inaccurate. Overall, comparing any predictive metric from your planning process with the corresponding retrospective measure from the completed work will help you decide which project processes to keep and which to fix.

Similarly, comparing your scope, final costs, and finish date with your committed project objectives may be a useful way to assess your processes overall. This is only helpful if your objectives were based on bottom-up, plan-based data, though. If your project objective was a wild guess or, even worse, a "stretch goal" yanked out of the air by some upper-level manager, you have a big "compared to what?" problem. If your project objectives were not credible, then project-level comparisons won't reveal much beyond the fact that you have inept high-level

247

management. Although the numbers can tell you a lot, project assessment is really about more than just achieving "scope, time, and cost."

Assessing Teamwork and Satisfaction

Most projects exist in a small world. A succession of projects will tend to be done with many of the same team members, for the same management, and in support of the same stakeholders and customers. Some indicators telling you how well you are doing from an interpersonal standpoint are objective measures, and some are more subjective evaluations.

A measurable indication of successful teaming is low turnover. For a particular project team this should be a relative measure, because people leave for many reasons. If your track record for retaining people is good compared with that of other project leaders, you are probably doing most things right. More subjective signs that you're an effective team leader are a minimum amount of "burnout" at the end of your projects, and a willingness on the part of your team members to work with you again on a future project.

Customer satisfaction is also important for successful project management. Some projects use a postdelivery survey to assess customer and stakeholder satisfaction. If you do this regularly, you can also track results over time. Other indicators showing that you are doing well are stakeholders who remain friendly and are still speaking with you at the end of the work, and customers who return to you with their next requests and new projects.

Your management and sponsor also get a vote. If your annual job appraisal is positive, it's likely that you are performing well. You can also tell something about the success of your projects from the comments, rewards, and recognition you (and your team) receive. If you are not getting much feedback from your management, approach it and request it—whether you are seen as doing well or not, it's always best to know.

100. What are good practices for ending a canceled project?

Not every project ends as planned. There are many reasons for projects to end prematurely, but there is value to be realized even when you can't deliver the results expected. It is often said that good project management comes from experience. Canceled projects are a rich source of experience, so you should use it. Also, you need to take care of the people who have been involved as your paths may cross again.

Documenting What Happened

Whenever a project ends early, assess the state of your deliverables and work with your stakeholders to determine if anything you have produced can be used as it is, or could become useful with small incremental effort. Turn over the deliverables (or partial deliverables) that you are able to finish, and request acknowledgment and approval from your stakeholders.

It's good practice to do a final project report for all projects, even ones that are canceled. Summarize what was accomplished in your report and name the individuals who contributed to your results. Objectively describe why it was decided to end the project, and provide a final status summary. Archive all your project data, updating plans and other documents to reflect your current status. Not only will this support your post-project analysis, but it will also facilitate possible resumption of the project down the road or any follow-on efforts that will benefit from your experiences.

Hold a post-project retrospective meeting, involving as many of your contributors as possible. If convincing people to participate proves to be difficult, take advantage of the ideas in Problem 101, emphasizing the opportunity to discuss what happened openly and put it behind you. In your analysis, start with processes that worked and results you were able to achieve, so you can benefit from them on future projects. Next, focus on identifying changes that might have enabled you and your team to better deal with problems and issues you ran into. Also document any significant risks encountered on your project that may affect other

249

work. Prioritize the changes you recommend and work to implement the best of them.

Recognizing Individual Accomplishments

Whatever the reasons for a project being canceled, meet individually with each person involved to thank him or her personally at the end of the project. If specific rewards and recognition are available and appropriate, seek or recommend them. For team members who work for others, send a note to their managers describing their performance and accomplishments, emphasizing the positive.

Also meet with your stakeholders and sponsor for a project debrief. Discuss expectations, met and unmet, and explore what you could do differently on a future project to ensure a better conclusion.

Even for projects that crash and burn, schedule and hold a small team event at the end. If your organization will not support it, fund it yourself or have a "pot luck" where everyone brings something along to eat and help celebrate. It's a small world, and it's quite likely you will work with the same people again. Strive to end things on a high note so that your next project will start without ill will or bad feelings.

101. How can I motivate contributors to participate in project retrospective analysis?

Once a project is finished, people tend to want to move on to the next thing. Also, assessing lessons learned requires yet another meeting, and most people hate meetings. To get past this, you'll need to supply a compelling answer to the question "What's in it for me?" If you have reluctant contributors, point out personal, project-oriented, and organizational benefits to gain their commitment to participate.

One definition of insanity is doing the same thing over and over expecting a different result. Project retrospectives are a powerful opportunity to find and change the things that lead to undesirable results.

Focusing on the Personal

Most projects have tension, crisis, drama, and at least a bit of chaos. One of the purposes of a project "postmortem" is to help people put this behind them and shed most of this baggage so they can approach their next undertakings with a good attitude and an open mind. Discussing what went well on a project highlights the positive, and it provides a good opportunity to give credit for achievements and accomplishments.

Discussing what could have gone better also can be constructive, especially if your intent is to identify needed changes. Confronting annoyances and problems openly provides catharsis, a release of feelings that people may be bottling up inside. Kept inside, they will affect attitudes and behavior. Simply providing an opportunity to voice them goes a long way toward diffusing emotions. Some things that come out may seem trivial in retrospect, and others may be things that you can easily change on future projects. People may feel better even about the things that appear out of your control after they have had a chance to discuss them. Your role as a project leader is to let all the participants vent and to keep everyone focused on the process and potential remedies instead of character assassination and "blamestorming."

Building Better Projects

The most frequently cited reason for post-project retrospective analyses is to capture lessons learned. If you analyze projects routinely and act upon what you discover, your next projects will be shorter and more efficient. This is better for everyone, because it will drive process improvements that will result in future projects with less chaos, frustration, and confusion. To make unenthusiastic team members more interested in meeting to capture lessons learned, commit to doing something about the primary recommendations that emerge from the meeting. Commit in advance to either act on them or propose their implementation to your management.

On a very large program where I was responsible for the retrospective analysis after each phased release, the program management team committed to implementing the top three recommended changes from each quarterly implementation. This resulted in broad and willing participation, and it led to substantially better overall control and a good deal less confusion. Most people will willingly participate if they know that their efforts will not be ignored.

Helping the Organization

Even at the organization level there can be significant benefits for the individual. Increased efficiency will lead to a healthier overall business, and success leads to better job security, growth, and opportunities for advancement. The benefits of disciplined post-project analysis also include organizational learning, and the work environment is more stable and a lot more pleasant when there is a solid base of intellectual capital. In addition, focusing on accomplishments and good results provides visibility for your contributors that can be used to identify new project leaders and subject matter experts for future projects.

Index

absence from project, managing, 176–177
accomplishments, recognizing, 91
action items
  assessing actual performance, 130–133
  holiday impact on duration, 134–135
  sequencing, 136–137
  status visibility, 166
activity-level estimating, 123–125
actual cost (AC), 132
adversaries, confronting, 59–60
agenda
  for launch meeting, 62–63
  for meetings, 92
  regional/cross-functional, reconciling competing, 56–58
aggregations of activity-level metrics, 131
agreement, on project objective, 10
alliances, 60–61
approach, choosing, 8–9
archiving information, 11, 66, 81
  for programs, 113
  prohibiting deletion, 82
around-the-clock staffing, 207
"as is" processes, preserving effective, 48
assignments, closing, 167
audit trail, for communications, 181
automatic version maintenance, 242
availability, assessing potential, 121

baseline
  management demands after setting, 212–213
  negotiating, 196–198
  protecting, 209
bidding for work, reasons to decline, 183
big projects, decomposing, 64–65, 115–116
bonding, with team members, 11
bottom-up estimates of costs, 125
Boy Scouts of America, 6
brainstorming, 222
budget for project, 44

canceled project, ending, 249–250
Capability Maturity Model Integration (CMMI), 14
certification in project management, 12–13
change
  analyzing and managing, 11
  anticipating, 48, 219
  assessing need for, 189
  and funding, 75
  making good decisions, 213
  managing, 215–216
  to meet project deadline, 187
  to objectives, 209–211
  planning, 189–190
  in schedule, 201–202
  securing buy-in, 149–150
  in software project, 34
change-control process, 210–211

253